THE CREDIT GAME MASTERY SERIES

EMPOWERING YOUR PERSONAL AND USINESS INANCES

CHEVON K. PATRICK

CONTENTS

THE CREDIT GAME

PLAYS WE WERE NEVER TAUGHT

CHEVON K. PATRICK

*I dedicate this book to those who wish to empower themselves and others.
America's wealth gap has been made worse by an education gap—a gap
between the financial education given to the children of the rich vs. the
children of the middle and working classes.
Many of us were never taught about credit or financial literacy. I know how
easily this can lead to disaster, and feelings of helplessness and hopelessness.
It doesn't have to be that way. We can all learn how to use the credit and
financial systems we are born into to our advantage and build wealth for our
communities.
This book is written to help you to accomplish just that.*

CHAPTER 1
THE CREDIT TRAP

There was a time when I knew nothing about credit. Like so many people, I knew that credit cards appeared to be free money, and frankly couldn't care less about what happened to my unpaid bills. With credit, I could spend money I did not actually have and unpaid debts afforded me more money on hand.

As a young teen mother struggling to survive, I could have access to experiences and material things that my minimum wage income did not allow for. Credit cards and spending beyond my means could give me a glimpse of a better life.

Most everybody I knew used credit cards this way: as a lifeline to a better future they would someday catch up to. I planned to pay my debts back *someday*.

But maybe my plan to pay them back wasn't as solid as I thought. And maybe, in the midst of being offered more and more free money, I lost track of how much I actually owed.

What was the worst that could happen? And an even better question, how come we weren't taught about credit in school?

I didn't know what my credit score was, and no one I knew ever mentioned credit. It was one of those things that we heard people talking about on TV, but which never actually became relevant in our lives.

Later, I would learn the long history of government policies that facilitated wealth for white Americans and not blacks. If we'd known more about credit and finance, we might not have felt the need to borrow money we could not repay. We might have actually *had* that life of ownership and wealth that we spent our time and credit dreaming of.

I had saved up enough money to start college, and borrowed several thousands more to pay the ongoing costs of tuition. I'd gotten good grades, following the pre-Recession wisdom of getting the most prestigious education I could under the assumption that this would pay massive financial dividends. Unfortunately, I also had the Recession to worry about. Like so many people, I found that the degree I had paid so much for did not pay me back as much as I'd been promised.

After graduation, I was in trouble. I had finally discovered the truth about credit scores at the worst possible time. The truth was, if you had a bad credit score, you could find yourself out on the street.

Landlords were running credit checks, and turning me down for housing when they saw my frightening credit score. I couldn't buy or rent a car without paying extortionary double-digit interest rates and heavy down payments because of my poor credit. I was even denied a promising job after a would-be employer ran a credit check and decided that my irresponsible financial history would make me a liability to their company.

These past years, as I'd been using alternative methods like dead end jobs, selling drugs, financial aid, government assistance, and credit cards to survive motherhood and college, I had borrowed money without paying it back. Now I was being told that I *couldn't* pay it back, because I was being denied employment and forced to take ultra-high-interest loans which cost far more than paying out of pocket with cash would have cost me.

This is the trap of poverty: it is *expensive* to be poor. Everything costs more when you can only afford to buy a little at a time. Everything costs more when you have to agree to high-interest loans instead of paying with cash or a good line of credit.

And this is the trap of credit cards: they *want* to lend you money, because they want to charge you interest and late fees. But the credit trap is one you can use to your advantage.

Credit card companies and credit bureaus must perform a delicate dance to stay in business. They must convince people to borrow money from them so that they can make money on interest and late fees. But they must also ensure that *most* people pay that money back, so that they don't take a huge net loss.

This is where our complicated credit system comes in. The financial system *wants* you to borrow money. But it only wants you to borrow what you can pay back soon. It rewards you for behaving this way: when you borrow money and then pay it back almost immediately, your credit score goes up. And the higher your credit score, the less interest you are charged on loans and the more money you can be allowed to borrow.

Properly used, credit can be a beautiful thing. An excellent credit score can open doors to home ownership, business loans, car owner-ship, and other ways to leverage huge amounts of cash you may never be able to earn otherwise at low interest rates. In this way, you can build wealth. You can obtain wealth through loans to invest in prop-erty, business, and education, allowing you to make more money than you ever could have using your own savings and your 9-5 job alone.

This is among the secrets that the wealthy know. It often isn't neces-sary to save huge quantities of money in order to acquire wealth. Instead, if you have a truly solid business plan, it is often possible to *borrow* large sums of money, and turn that money into a much larger sum than you originally borrowed through your sound investment.

But that's only possible if you have a good credit score, and the access to good lines of credit that brings. If you *don't* have that, you can instead find yourself actively punished in areas ranging from housing to employment for failing to demonstrate that you can borrow money and then pay it back.

In my early 20s, it seemed like I was doomed. I had all kinds of debts, bills, and felt like I'd never get ahead. And with employers checking my credit report before deciding whether to hire me, it seemed as though I wouldn't be able to get a good paying job to pay off my debts until after I'd paid off my debts. It was a Catch-22. And I had a child to support: failure was not an option.

I began to research the problem. How exactly had my credit score gotten so bad? That was simple: by charging money on credit cards and not paying it back, not paying my bills on time or at all, and carelessly dismissing my student loans.

But how did I fix it? That was more complicated. It involved not only paying my debts, but also navigating a complicated maze of letter-writing, credit monitoring, interest rate calculations, and numerous other complex and time-consuming tasks.

But there was a silver lining: the fact that these tasks existed meant that there was something I could do. I didn't have to just wait for money to magically appear and hope my credit score got better. So I threw myself into doing the things I learned about through my research. I threw myself into it with a passion.

Slowly but surely, I began to see progress. I learned from many iterations of trial and error, where I tried something that just plain didn't work or even made the situation *worse*. I'll share my mistakes with you in this book, so you won't have to make them all yourself.

By 2014, I was able to finance a newer Nissan Maxima. In 2016, my heart sang as I closed on ownership of my first home—a four-bedroom house with a low-interest fixed-rate mortgage and only paid $422 out of my pocket on the closing date!

My home ownership was possible because of the way I had built up my credit score, and learned to use credit to grow my wealth instead of growing debts, over the preceding years. I'd gone from being a broke single mom struggling through college to a four-bedroom homeowner with big plans to continue growing generational wealth for my family. I had essentially jumped straight from one socioeconomic class to another.

And without my credit education, this would never have been possible.

In this book, I want to teach you everything I learned during those years of struggle. I will even supply you with letter templates, phone scripts, and a list of vetted and reliable tools to use to repair, protect, and build your credit so that you can do the same to establish your own wealth.

We will close this book with a brief discussion of business credit—a tool that is different from personal credit, but which can be used for the same astonishing wealth-building purposes, and which most people never learn anything about.

All I ask is that you read through this book carefully, and apply any of its techniques which might improve your fortunes. I want you to succeed and build wealth as I have done. If the necessary steps prove too time-consuming or difficult for where you are right now, my business can help you with the labor.

Together, we can change your destiny.

CHAPTER 2
HOW CAN I BENEFIT FROM CREDIT?

Your credit score is very much like your track record in a competitive sport. An expert on the game can glance at somebody's credit history and know exactly how good they are at playing the credit game. A credit expert can estimate that person's chances of winning in specific circumstances because they can see what challengers they've already faced and how they fared.

This is important, because the better a bank or creditor thinks you are at the game, the more money they will give you. Now it's not a free gift—you have to pay it back. But how *much* you have to pay back, and how much you're given in the first place, will largely depend on your credit score.

Say, for example, you want to buy a house. To do this, on paper, you need $300,000, because that's how much the house costs. Obviously not a lot of people have $300,000 lying around. But someone with an excellent credit score could get a $300,000 mortgage, which will allow them to live in the house and claim ownership while they gradually pay the house off over time. The same holds true for business loans, cars, and countless other forms of credit.

In fact, it's a little-known truth that the very wealthy rarely spend their own money to make money—they typically use their excellent credit scores to take out mortgages and loans, which they can use their business knowledge to turn into much, much more money than they borrowed in the first place. This is how they become wealthy.

And this is what my series of books are designed to teach you to do.

Now don't jump the gun and immediately go out and procure a massive loan which you try to turn a profit on. The only reason the very wealthy are able to succeed in this is that:

1. They have excellent credit, and;
2. They have insider knowledge of how to identify and use profitable investments. You *can* gain this knowledge, but it will take an excellent credit score and probably also a few years unless you have a mentor to fast-track the process. Think of this as a long game. If you are ambitious about making massive wins, you have to make your early moves carefully and strategically.

Why is having excellent credit so important before you try to grow your wealth with mortgages or business loans? Well, your credit score will impact your interest payment.

When asked what the most powerful force in the universe was, Albert Einstein is widely reported to have said "compound interest." That probably wasn't the answer the interviewer was expecting from a physicist, but it goes to show how powerful interest rates can be. "Compound interest" refers to the amount of money you pay—or *get* paid—over time as a consequence of someone borrowing money.

The trick about interest rates is that they often look tiny. The difference between a good interest rate and a bad interest rate may be just a few percent of the total amount you are borrowing. You may look at that few percent and think, "I can afford to pay that."

But the trick is, the way that interest adds up over time when it is applied monthly or yearly to your loan or mortgage comes out to be much more than a few percent. On that $300,000 house I mentioned earlier, having a high interest rate might mean you end up paying a full $99,000 more for the same property than you would have paid if you'd had a lower interest rate!

This is how the rich get richer and those of us who aren't rich, all too often, get poorer.

But the good news is, you don't need to be rich to have an excellent credit score and get excellent interest rates. Anyone can do it. You just need to know how.

Just like any competitive sport, having a great credit track record is a learned skill. How good you get at the game is determined by the amount of time, effort, and strategy you put into winning.

In this chapter we'll investigate the underlying logic of credit scores —how banks and creditors decide how much money to lend you, how they decide what interest rates to charge, and why they think any of that is a good idea. This underlying logic will help us understand the specific steps we need to take to get into the same credit tier as the ultra-wealthy.

WHY LEND MONEY AT ALL?

At this point you might be asking yourself, "Why would banks and creditors lend money at all? What's in it for them?" After all, we're rarely thrilled when a friend or family member comes and asks us to lend them cash.

The answer to that question is the most powerful force in the universe: interest.

Suppose you're a bank or creditor. You lend a lot of money to a lot of different people. And all of those people end up paying you back *more* than you leant them, because you charge interest. What looks like just a few percent interest on that $300,000 mortgage means you get paid $99,000 more than you leant out over time. And you may be making such loans to hundreds of thousands or even millions of people if you're a big lender.

Essentially, the more money you lend, the more money you make, usually. This is why banks are such powerful financial players.

But this puts you in something of a competition with borrowers.

Borrowers want you to lend them money so they can live in that $300,000 house, and someday maybe sell it to get $300,000 or more in cash without having to put up $300,000 cash up front. But they *don't* want to be charged $99,000 in interest. They want to get the lowest interest rate possible.

They do this by having an excellent credit score. Here's why and how that works.

Remember when I noted above that the more money you lend, the more money you make as a bank or creditor? But I appended a "usually." That "usually" comes from the fact that a certain percentage of borrowers won't pay back the money they borrow. This represents a loss for the bank or creditor. Obviously, banks wish to avoid such losses.

They do this by measuring how good a person is at paying back money they borrow. If someone frequently fails to pay their bills, the banks must try to cover their potential losses from that person by charging them a sky-high credit rate. This can even be profitable if the bank actually gets many people to pay these sky-high credit rates over time.

If someone always pays their bills promptly, on the other hand, the equation changes. This is someone who a bank or creditor can be pretty sure will pay back what they're leant. This means this person can be offered a much lower interest rate without risk to the bank. And, more importantly, it means the bank *has* to offer them a lower interest rate.

Why? Because everybody wants to lend money to these repayment superstars. Their excellent credit means they are virtually guaranteed to pay back what they borrow, with interest. That means that every bank and credit card out there is competing to lend these people money and get it paid back with just a little bit of interest. Whoever offers the lowest interest rate may just be the one to capture that person's business.

By paying bills promptly on time and knowing other techniques to ensure your credit score is as high as possible, you become one of the borrowers that banks and creditors compete with each other to lend to.

You have such a good track record at the credit game that different "teams"—banks or creditors—will make you competing offers to try to get you to play for them.

If you have a poor credit score, on the other hand, you might suffer the classic tragedy of that unathletic kid on the playground: you might get picked for the team last, and given all the worst positions to play.

The unfortunate side effect of this system is that it often favors the wealthy—those who already have so much money that paying the bills is not a challenge for them—while harming those living in poverty, forcing them to pay much more for pretty much everything they might desire to possess via high interest rates.

The good news is, we can fix your interest rate and make you a credit superstar no matter how little money you have. In this game, strategy is even more important than raw power. Let's start learning how to do that now.

HOW TO BUILD YOUR CREDIT SCORECARD

If you were a coach deciding what players to hire for your team, what factors might you look at? You might look at things like:

- How many games they had won in the past.
- How many teams they had played for successfully.
- How frequently they screwed up, costing the team points.

This is quite similar to how banks and creditors evaluate you as a borrower. The exact formula used to determine a FICO credit score—the most common credit score used by banks and creditors to determine whether to lend you money, and at what interest rate—goes something like this:

1. Payment history. This is basically your track record for winning games. A bill paid on time is a credit game won. A bill paid over 30 days late or not at all is a game lost. The more games you've won in the past, the more a bank or creditor wants you to play for their team. And the more they are willing to "pay" in terms of low interest rates

and other financial rewards to get you on their team. Payment history accounts for about 35% of your credit score.

One important thing to note here is that you can't win any games if you don't play. Some people assume they must have perfect credit because they have never borrowed money. If you never spend more money than you need, that's a really good sign for your financial responsibility, right?

But in the eyes of banks and creditors, the opposite is true. If no one has ever seen you pick up a ball, they're not just going to assume that you can make breathtaking plays. So you've got to borrow money and pay it back—you've got to play the game—in order to build credit. The key is to borrow money, not because you *need* to, but because you are doing it strategically to optimize your credit score.

We'll discuss the details of how to do this later.

2. Amounts owed. If someone owes a lot of money, that's not a great sign for you as a lender. *Why* do they owe so much money? Why haven't they paid more of it back yet? If I lend them money, are they going to be able to pay me back *and* pay back all these other people?

Think of this like a sports team hiring someone who they know already has a full-time commitment to another team. How much time and energy is that player really going to be able to give your team? You want someone who isn't overcommitted, and who you know has a lot of free time and energy to give your team a stellar performance.

As a borrower, you want to keep your credit utilization rate below 30%. That means that of the total amount of money you are allowed to charge on your credit card, for example, you're only using 30% or less. In general, lower is better. The more credit you have that you're not using, the more time and energy you have available to devote to any other team you apply for, so to speak. Having that availability makes you a better candidate.

This metaphor will break down a little bit in a minute, but for now that's a useful way to think of it.

Amounts owed—the less, the better—makes up about 30% of your credit score.

3. Credit history length. The more games you've played and won,

the better you look to a sports team. The longer you've been borrowing money and paying it back successfully, the better you look to a bank or creditor.

This is why it's so important to start building credit history with a credit card or loan *as soon as possible*. The longer you make payments successfully, the better your credit score gets over time.

But don't go out and get any old loan or credit card right now! In the chapters to come, I will share some specific credit card and loan options that offer great benefits to people with low credit scores which will allow you to start building positive lines of credit and gain maximum benefits.

Learning which loans and cards will help vs. hurt your credit and finances is an integral part of the game strategy. Read just a few more chapters to learn to improve your credit score without paying interest rates to profit somebody else.

4. Credit mix. This is where the sports metaphor breaks down a little. When hiring an athlete, you usually want that athlete to be playing *only* for your team. But banks and creditors want you to have *multiple* creditors, if only so that you can prove that you're already paying multiple accounts successfully.

Think of it like if sports had an option to keep a player on retainer. This player is not being called upon often enough to negatively impact their ability to perform for you, but the fact that so many teams want him—and the fact that they perform well for all of them—makes you really, really want him on your team.

Banks and creditors like to see that you regularly pay a variety of different types of bills. They like you to have a loan or two under your belt, as well as multiple credit cards.

This is a dangerous mix for someone who isn't very good at budgeting; they could easily use all these sources of borrowed money to get deeply in debt with no way out. But that's precisely what proves your skill to creditors; if you can juggle that many accounts and win every time, you must be really really excellent.

Think of a player who wins games for five different teams, reliably, every single month. If that person went looking for another team to join wouldn't you really want them? Wouldn't you offer them a super-great paycheck—or interest rate and rewards package—to join you?

Credit mix makes up about 10% of your credit score.

5. New credit. Let's extend the sports metaphor here: if a player *just* started playing for a bunch of new teams in a short span of time, you'd be kind of nervous about them, wouldn't you? What if they've over-committed? What if they can't perform well for all of you at the same time, and they just haven't figured that out yet?

Opening a lot of new lines of credit, or attempting to do so, is a red flag for lenders. It suggests that you might be having a lot of trouble paying bills, or might be trying to borrow more money than you can feasibly pay back.

This can be especially frustrating, because shopping around for just a single loan can *look* like you're applying for too many lines of credit —or *not*, depending on how strategically you act. This once happened to me: I only needed one loan, but because of the way I went about applying for one, it looked to my creditors like I was seeking *dozens* of loans. My credit score took a big hit because of that.

We will explore how to be strategic in applying for new lines of credit, to ensure you get the loan you need without sending out multiple applications that raise red flags for lenders, later in this book.

Your number of recent credit applications make up about 10% of your FICO score.

Having read this description, perhaps you now have a better idea of just how important strategy is to the credit game. Having wealth already in your pocket is the easiest way to make sure you pay your bills on time, but decisions about which bills to pay first, how to strate-gically use your existing lines of credit, when to borrow money and from whom, and how to apply for loans you need can all make your credit score better—or worse.

In this way, someone with lots of money but little knowledge of the game can end up with less borrowing power and higher interest rates than someone with little disposable income but excellent strategic knowledge. If you play strategically, you can end up with the kinds of mortgages and business loans that build a legacy of generational wealth for your family, even if you have little to no cash.

Now that we understand how banks and creditors evaluate us as players, let's learn exactly how to play the game.

CHAPTER 3
WINNING AT PAYMENT HISTORY

THE VERY FIRST thing many people need to tackle is improving their payment history. Poor payment history happens when you have credit cards, loans, or other bills that you have paid late or not at all. Any type of creditor including doctors and hospitals, universities and student loan companies, and many others can report you to credit bureaus in a way that harms your credit score if you don't pay them.

Any of them *can*. But not all of them *do*. That's one aspect of credit strategy.

Obviously, if you had a ton of money you wouldn't be having problems with payment history in the first place. This can make tackling this problem particularly daunting, because it's not like you're not paying simply because you don't feel like it. If you could magically produce enough money to pay all of these bills, you would have done it already.

So what we're going to talk about here is how to strategize to pay the bills which are hurting you most *first*. Eventually, we will want to pay all of them; but the more high-impact bills we take care of, the easier it will become to take care of the rest. We'll consider factors like:

- Interest rates. Are you paying way more money in interest on some bills than others? If so, we'll take care of those bills first so that you're charged less money in interest. That will free up more money to pay other bills.
- Late fees. Are you accruing late fees or other penalties on certain types of bills? These will eat into your overall budget and make it harder to pay off anything at all. So we'll also take care of those first.
- Credit score impact. Are some of your creditors harming your credit score more than others? If so, we will prioritize those. You may even be able to open low interest rate lines of credit that you can use to help pay off or consolidate your other bills. This can help get your credit score up by removing negative items from your report.
- Seven-year statutory limit. Did you know that most derogatory marks on your credit report should be removed after a period of seven years? This may be very important for you if you have outstanding debts which are five or more years old. You may not need to pay these in order for them to disappear.

Attacking your payment history strategically will allow you to save a lot of money compared to simply randomly paying whatever creditor is being most insistent at a given time. That in turn will make it easier for you to get a stellar payment history quickly. So let's get started.

THE STATUTORY LIMIT

One of the most important things to know in the credit game is that all negative reporting has a statutory limit. This means that a negative item cannot remain on your credit report for more than a certain period of time.

Most of the time, this makes little difference: if you have negative items on your credit report and you wish to buy a house, rent an apartment, apply for a business loan, buy or lease a car, or get a job which requires a credit check *before* the seven-year statutory limit occurs, you will want to resolve these negative items and/or pursue options to raise your credit score immediately such as those we discuss here. But there are also times when you can use the statutory limit to your advantage.

If a negative item on your credit report is already six years old and you owe a lot of money on that bill, it might make sense to simply wait for it to fall off your report before making a major financial move or trying to contact that company. If *not* paying this bill means saving tens of thousands of dollars, waiting a few months for that derogatory mark to disappear may make more sense than paying.

One other piece of information that is vital to know is this: if you contact your creditor about your debt, you restart the age of the account. This means that the clock starts counting down from "zero" again, and it will take seven years *after the last date of activity.*

This is why it's important to pay attention to the age of your accounts before taking action on them. If an account of yours is already five or six years old, contacting the creditor to pay or negotiate may result in losing your ability to have the red mark automatically removed from your report in just one or two years without the necessity to pay.

Keep this in mind when filling out the following chapters, which will invite you to make a strategy to pay off your outstanding debts while saving as much money as possible. If a debt is already six years old and you don't need your credit history improved immediately in the next few months, you can omit that debt from your calculations as it should soon automatically disappear from your credit report on its own.

KNOW YOUR INTEREST RATES

If you have taken out multiple loans, there's a good chance they have different interest rates. Do you know what your interest rate is on each loan, mortgage, and credit card you have? If not, I want you to go through your files and look up that information right now. Here's a little worksheet you can fill out so we can keep track:

Credit Line 1: _______________________________________

    Interest rate: ______% **Amount owed:** ________________________

    Credit Line 2: ___________________________________

    Interest rate: ______% **Amount owed:** ________________________

    Credit Line 3: ___________________________________

    Interest rate: ______% **Amount owed:** ________________________

    Credit Line 4: ___________________________________

    Interest rate: ______% **Amount owed:** ________________________

    Credit Line 5: ___________________________________

    Interest rate: ______% **Amount owed:** ________________________

    Credit Line 6: ___________________________________

Interest rate: ______% **Amount owed:** ________________________

Now, here's a bit of simple math: the higher the interest rate on any given credit line, the more money that loan is costing you for every single month there remains a balance. This is very significant, especially since paying that interest over time might be stopping you from paying *other* bills, which might in turn be causing you more interest and late fees.

This is what I refer to as "the interest snowball." When you are paying more than necessary in interest, this cost can end up multiplying and costing you way more than you realize in interest payments and late fees over time.

In order to get your interest payments down, we're going to prioritize paying off your highest-interest lines of credit *first*. The moment those lines of credit are fully paid, poof—your interest payments disappear!

Now, you don't want to stop paying other bills entirely in order to pay off a high-interest line of credit. But you might consider going down to the minimum payment you can make without being punished with late fees or interest rate hikes on other lines of credit in order to put as much money as possible toward making the highest-interest debt disappear.

You might also consider temporarily cutting down on unnecessary expenses in order to achieve this. There may be pleasures you would not want to go without permanently, but if skipping them for a few weeks allows you to eliminate a high-interest loan, you can think of the temporary deprivation as an investment in having a lot more spending money in the future.

Let's take a moment to rank your open credit lines by interest rate, in order from highest to lowest. Place the loan with the highest interest rate at the top of the list, and the loan with the lowest interest rate at the bottom:

Credit Line 1: _______________________ **Interest Rate:** _____%

Credit Line 2: _______________________ **Interest Rate:** _____%

Credit Line 3: _______________________ **Interest Rate:** _____%

Credit Line 4: _______________________ **Interest Rate:** _____%

Credit Line 5: _______________________ **Interest Rate:** _____%

Credit Line 6: _______________________ **Interest Rate:** _____%

Now, focus on getting each of these lines of credit completely paid off as quickly as possible, moving from top to bottom. This will save you the most money in the long run, and saving money means having money available to make credit power moves.

While you're eliminating high-interest lines of credit that you already owe, it's also a good idea to start comparatively shopping in the event that you need to open a new line of credit for some reason.

It's a good idea to avoid taking out a new loan or line of credit at this time, because if you wait a few weeks or months until we have implemented the other steps in this workbook you will get much better offers. But if you simply must take out a new loan or line of credit, follow this protocol to get the best results:

1. Research until you find at least *six* different options that are available to you to procure this financing.
2. Of the six options you find, carefully review their terms and interest rates.
3. Choose the option with the *lowest* interest rate to add to your credit roster.

Again, I would advise waiting until you have worked all the way through this book to ensure that you get the best possible terms and make the most strategic plays. But if life happens in the meantime, be conscious of the terms you are agreeing to and the fact that there are always multiple financing options available to you.

KNOW YOUR LATE FEES & OVERDRAFT FEES

Late fees are another way we can lose more money than we realize. These often come out to cost us less than interest rates because they are typically small, flat, fixed fees. But paying several late fees can add up to over $100 per month *just* going to late fees, and not helping you afford anything you want!

Late fees can also apply to things that interest rates typically don't, such as late fees on rent payments. Some creditors may charge *both* interest rates and late fee payments, which can add up very quickly.

For each line of credit or monthly bill that you are struggling to pay, look up what your fee for late payment is and list them here. This will help tell you what bills you should prioritize paying first if you can't pay all of them on time in order to save the most money:

Bill 1: ____

Late fee amount: ______$ **Kicks in after what date?** ___/___/______

Bill 2: ____

Late fee amount: ______$ **Kicks in after what date?** ___/___/______

Bill 3: ____

Late fee amount: _______$ **Kicks in after what date?**
___/___/_______

Bill 4: ____

Late fee amount: _______$ **Kicks in after what date?**
___/___/_______

Bill 5: ____

Late fee amount: _______$ **Kicks in after what date?**
___/___/_______

Bill 6: ____

Late fee amount: _______$ **Kicks in after what date?**
___/___/_______

Keep these amounts and dates in mind, and try to strategically balance your budget to avoid having to pay any late fees. If this requires short term sacrifices, remember that your finances will grow more and more powerful as you eliminate late fees and interest payments from the amount you are paying each month moving into the future.

There is one final, very important consideration to take into account when prioritizing which bills to pay first. This is a factor that can work powerfully for you or against you if you use it properly.

KNOW WHO IS REPORTING TO THE CREDIT BUREAUS

What if I told you that not every single party you owe money to may report you to a credit bureau? It's not a good idea to plan to skip out on bills, but if you are overwhelmed with debt and need to pay down your most pressing debts fast, knowing which, if any of your creditors will not negatively impact your credit score can be very powerful.

The best way to know which bills are or are not harming your credit score is to check your credit report. Your credit report will show exactly which creditors have reported you as late-paying or non-paying, harming your credit track record. Some creditors will report you quickly and aggressively, even if you only owe them a tiny amount; others, for various reasons, may elect not to do so even if you owe them thousands of dollars.

If a negative remark appears on your credit report, sometimes you can quickly raise your credit score by paying that bill. But first, you will need to call the creditor and specifically request that they report a change in your payment status to the credit bureau. Be sure to get this agreement in writing! Once they agree, if you get the payment status reported properly, it is as though your late payment or nonpayment never happened.

If you can catch a late bill while it's still in collections before it hits your credit file, that's even better. In that case, you can sometimes negotiate payment for pennies on the dollar!

Now, you've solved the nonpayment problem, so that loss is removed from your scorecard and replaced by a win. We will cover exactly how to make this happen later in this book.

Since the only way to be certain which bills are harming your credit score is to look at your credit report, let's investigate how to do that next.

CHAPTER 4
CHECKING YOUR CREDIT REPORT

There are many services out there which claim to offer free access to your credit score and credit report. While some of these can be helpful, unfortunately, not all of them are reliable enough to be your primary source of information.

As with any bureaucratic system, mistakes can creep into the process of calculating a credit report. For this reason, third party reports offered by sites like Credit Karma and Credit Sesame may not actually match what potential landlords, employers, and lenders will see when they file a formal credit check to make a decision about whether to allow you to rent a property, take out a mortgage or business loan, or any number of countless essential operations that can be affected by your credit score.

Here are some of my favorite sources for accurate information about your credit score, and what nonpayment items might be negatively affecting it. Once you have this information, you can target these negative items for repair.

ANNUALCREDITREPORT.COM

AnnualCreditReport.com is the official website to check your credit report. This website is actually regulated by the government, which requires that it provide a free credit report to everyone at least once per year. During emergency times like the COVID-19 pandemic, the government may even mandate that free scores be made available to people more frequently to allow them to stay on top of their credit during times of economic upheaval.

That's how important credit reports are: free access to them is considered a fundamental right that is protected by the government. And the government *must* mandate that they be made freely available at least once per year, because they are valuable enough that many people would pay for access.

As of this writing, all three credit bureaus are offering free credit reports on a weekly basis instead of an annual one due to the economic hardship posed by COVID-19. Since we cannot guarantee that will last forever, I will write the rest of this chapter with the assumption that the credit bureaus will eventually revert to offering these scores only once per year.

One important thing to know is that you *don't* have to pay for access to your credit report once per year. Some credit bureau websites may display misleading messages implying that you can't see your credit score or report at all unless you subscribe to a paid service. This is not the case: if you go to a website and receive such a message, hunt around until you find a link that allows you to go to your free credit report instead. This must be offered to you freely. It is a federal requirement.

The fact that, in typical times, the government only requires that you be offered your credit report freely once per year can be an impediment to some people. How are we to know if our credit building efforts are working if we can only access our reliable report once per year?

Well, there's good news: there are three different bureaus which provide FICO credit score estimates to banks, landlords, employers, etc. And you get to access *each one* for free once per year. That means that, if you only check one at a time, you can check one report every four months for free.

The three major bureaus which provide credit estimates to potential lenders are Equifax, Experian, and Transunion. Each of these organizations use proprietary formulas to try to calculate your FICO score based on the credit score factors we've discussed so far. Their reports may slightly differ from each other because of the different algorithms and/or accounts reporting, but the scores usually come out to be within a few points of each other across all three bureaus.

Now, just knowing your credit score does not do much if you don't know what specific unpaid bills may be harming it. Your credit report, when you access it through AnnualCreditReport.com, will list in detail *all* negative marks against your credit history.

It will list information about what creditor reported each negative mark, and that is the information you need: once you know who has reported you to a credit bureau for nonpayment, you know who you have to talk to and pay off or challenge ASAP to get the loss on your scorecard turned into a win.

To get started, why don't you get online and access your credit report right now? Access it for *only* one of the three bureaus, so that you will be able to access the other two later in the year.

When you open your credit report, you may see a list of complex acronyms indicating different types of problems that a credit report can have. Don't panic: that's not a list of all the problems with *your* report. It's a key so you can understand any problems that may appear on your report. Scroll down to see your personal credit history.

If you access your credit report through one of the three bureau websites, you can access a screen which will show your current credit score with that bureau, as well as a list of any late payments, debt collections, or other problems that have been reported to the credit bureau. This is the list you can use to address each of these negative marks and change your credit status to "paid as agreed." We will address some specific steps you can take to do this in a later chapter.

You may also see things on your credit report that don't make sense. Perhaps there are some accounts reported that definitely don't belong to you. This can happen for two reasons:

- There was a paperwork error involving someone with a similar name. People who share a first and last name with a close relative are especially prone to such errors.
- Your identity was stolen. In this case, someone managed to access enough of your personal, confidential information to open accounts while pretending to be you.

In both cases, there are solutions you can apply to get these incorrect items removed from your credit report. We'll discuss how to do this in a later chapter, too.

Are you comfortable with your credit report? If so, make a list of any problems reported in your report such as late payments or non-payments. Like the lists we made in the previous chapter, this will function as a master list to help you decide who to pay or challenge first. The faster you address these debts, the sooner you can turn these losses into wins on your scorecard.

Since larger debts don't necessarily harm your credit score more, you may wish to start by paying off small debts that appear on your credit report immediately and work your way up. Getting a $30 late utility bill paid off and removed from your credit report can be a very liberating feeling!

Problem 1: ____

Problem 2: ____

Problem 3: ____

Problem 4: ____

Problem 5: ____

Problem 6: ____

Now that we have opened the box that is your credit report, we will briefly discuss the other factors in addition to payment history that affect your credit report. Then we will investigate specific tools to get your payment status changed to "paid as agreed" and to dispute incorrect red marks on your credit score.

CHAPTER 5
WINNING CREDIT HISTORY LENGTH

When you're considering hiring a new player for your team, you want as much evidence as possible that they can help your team. If the player has played many games in the past, that gives you a lot of opportunity to see how they perform.

In the game of credit, we can think of the number of months of credit history under your belt as the number of games you have played. That means that someone with five or ten years of experience paying off credit lines under their belt is more likely to be picked for the good "teams"—or in this case, the good mortgages, credit cards, and car loans—than someone with few or no months of credit history under their belt.

If you haven't played many games of repayment before, how can banks have confidence that you have what it takes to pay off a $300,000 house? The answer is, they can't. And they probably won't lend you enough money to buy such a house.

This means that to create the best possible opportunities for yourself, you want to start building your credit history right now. This means finding a loan, a credit card, or both that you can pay off regularly each month to get some wins on your record.

Now, you don't want just *any* loan or credit card. As we discussed in the last chapter, some credit cards and loans offer excellent terms such that you lose nothing by using them. Others are downright predatory, with interest rates and enforcement terms that can easily harm your credit in the long run.

So how do you find a really good "team" to play for if you don't already have a lot of credit history to prove you're a good player? The good news is, there are loans and credit cards created specifically to help new players like yourself. Here are some of the best options.

To build credit history fast, you'll want to start playing for 3-5 different "teams" ASAP. This allows you to "win" 3-5 games each month, which shows banks and credit card companies that you're good at repaying the money you borrow on time.

We'll spend the rest of this chapter talking about my three favorite "teams" for new players to start with. If you do all three, you'll start building credit fast while paying little to no interest and with no risk of losing your assets.

RENTREPORTERS.COM

There's a good chance you're already paying rent to a landlord. It may surprise you to learn that these payments are *not* reported to credit bureaus. This can be a good thing or a bad thing, depending on your situation: if you struggle to pay rent on time, that won't harm your credit score. But it also means that all your on-time payments don't *help* your credit score. Unless you use RentReporters.com

This website allows you to sign up to have your monthly on-time rent payments reported as "wins" to the credit bureaus. If you are making rent payments on time and think you will be able to keep doing so for at least the next year, this is an excellent tool because it builds credit history without adding any new bills at all to your life. You simply get credit for the bills you're already paying.

If you don't pay rent because you own your home and you have a mortgage, good news: your mortgage payments are *already* being reported as "wins" to credit bureaus because they technically count as repayments on the money you agreed to pay the bank when you bought the property.

If you have been struggling to pay rent on time, or think you might struggle to do so in the next year, that is the only reason to *avoid* signing up for this service. We want to report wins on your record, so if you aren't certain of winning at paying rent, keep that particular game off your scorecard.

Whether you sign up for RentReporter.com or not, these following options can help you build your credit without the cost and risk associated with typical credit cards or loans.

CREDITBUILDERCARD.COM

CreditBuilderCard.com offers what is called a secured line of credit. A "secured" line means that you can get it even if you have a very poor credit score, because you promise to use the value of something you already own to pay the credit card company if you can't pay them back on time through normal means.

Most secured lines of credit can be very risky. Some secured credit lines may ask you to use things like your house or your retirement fund as "security," basically obligating you to give them these assets if you can't pay your bill. This is obviously very risky if you're agreeing to a huge amount of security in exchange for a line of credit.

However, CreditBuilderCard.com is built specifically to offer credit lines to people with poor credit scores without a big risk. For the Credit Builder card, the "security" you promise is just a one-time $200 deposit that you pay, which Credit Builder will use to cover any losses they may incur if you spend money on your credit card and can't pay it back.

The great thing about this is that they don't do a "hard inquiry"—a type of background check used by most lenders and credit card companies. This is important because hard inquiries actually hurt your credit score. This is because credit bureaus may assume that applying for credit cards or loans means you are struggling to pay your bills as-is, so they deduct a few points from your score each time you do so.

CreditBuilderCard.com does *not* run this kind of background check, so you will not lose those points by applying to open an account with them. In fact, none of the resources listed in this chapter run such inquiries, which means you can open three lines of credit to start "winning" three games every single month fast without losing any points to inquiries, the way you would if you applied for a normal commercial credit card or loan.

Now, CreditBuilderCard.com *does* report to major credit bureaus like any other credit card. That means that, just like RentReporter.com, your credit score may actually be harmed if you make purchases with your Credit Builder card and then don't pay your bill for this credit card on time.

The good news is, you choose how much you spend on this card and how much you subsequently have to pay back. I recommend simply charging a small expense like a meal or a cup of coffee on your Credit Builder card once a month or once every couple of months. This ensures that you will be able to win your credit game every single month by successfully making a payment for the full amount you owe.

One useful thing to know is that, when it comes to credit cards, credit bureaus don't care if you are paying back $25 or $500—both count as an equal repayment win, assuming that you have met the minimum payment requirement and stayed below 10% of your total credit card limit and you actually do pay the full amount off on time.

Because large and small payments both count as equal victories in the eyes of credit bureaus, it pays to use your credit card for just a tiny monthly purchase until you have built up the kind of credit score that allows you to have a high credit limit and an excellent interest rate if you don't pay off your full balance each month.

This next option is similar to CreditCardBuilder.com in its benefits for your credit score. It comes with the added cost of a fixed monthly payment, but also the added benefit that you get all the money you pay this lender back at the end of your "loan"!

SELFLENDER.COM

SelfLender.com is an ingenious idea built specifically to help people build credit without losing money. SelfLender.com combines the credit history benefits of taking out a loan with the money-saving benefits of a savings account.

First, you apply for a loan through the SelfLender.com website. Next, you choose how much to "borrow" and how long you want to take to "repay" the amount. I'm putting "borrow" and "repay" in quotation marks because you won't actually be borrowing or repaying anything; instead, you will be making payments into what is essentially a savings account.

Your payments to this savings account will be reported to credit bureaus as though you were paying off a loan. As long as you meet your savings goals and make the payments required by the contract you chose, you will be marked down as having a loan repayment win for the month.

But instead of getting money up-front which you then have to pay back, SelfLender.com essentially does things in reverse. You get the money you've paid into your savings account at the *end* of the process, and you don't have to pay it back since it is your money that you've saved up.

Pretty good deal, right? You get to build credit history with no hard inquiry, and at the end of the process you get paid a bunch of money that you have saved up for yourself through your monthly payments.

One of the best parts of the design is that, since you have not actually borrowed money that you are now obligated to pay back, you can cancel your account and stop paying off your "loan" at any time if you need to. This means that if something happens and you can't save up the full amount you planned, your credit score won't show this as a failure. Instead of taking losses on your scorecard for each month you can't pay, you'll simply show as taking a break from the game for personal reasons.

This tool builds your credit *and* your savings with none of the usual costs or risks associated with taking out a loan. There's no reason not to do it, and every reason to apply for an account today.

Remember, you'll be building skill at saving money in addition to building credit history. The money you save by paying yourself through SelfLender.com can even be used to pay off other lines of credit once you finish paying off your loan and the money you've paid in is returned to you.

KIKOFF.COM

KikOff.com is the last credit booster tool we'll be discussing in this chapter. Here you can sign up for an account and instantly get approved for a $500 line of credit. This is another provider that does not do a hard inquiry to check your scorecard, which means that applying with them will not cause your score to lose points. They do not require a minimum credit score and are an interest-free service with no additional fees.

KikOff.com also offers financial wellness ebooks and other self-help products with price tags starting between $10-$20. Their products require a minimum monthly payment of about only $2 per month which keeps their program affordable and easily manageable. They report each monthly payment to the three major credit bureaus. Each purchase helps build your credit month after month.

I often recommend that my clients set up a Visa gift card with at least $25 on it, then set their KikOff account to autopay from this gift card. This way you don't have to think about making your monthly payments—they are automatically withdrawn from your gift card—but you also don't get surprise charges on your primary bank account which may result in overdraft fees.

If you choose to use this approach, just ensure that you check back often enough to ensure that the Visa gift card remains loaded so you don't accidentally miss a payment!

NOW YOU'RE WINNING

If you use all three of these options, you will have three of the 3-5 lines of credit recommended by credit bureaus to build credit fast! And you will have done it all without losing any points to hard inquiries or taking on the risks of a high interest rate or a loan you can't pay back. Excellent work!

As your credit score rises as a result of meeting your commitments to pay rent, pay off that monthly cup of coffee you charge on your credit card, and pay yourself a few bucks each month in savings, you will find that you begin to qualify for better and better interest rates on loans and credit cards. This means you'll pay less money back for any money you borrow to buy a car or home or start a business.

You'll also qualify to borrow more and more money at a time as you demonstrate that you are capable of paying back what you borrow. This will allow you to have more robust emergency credit cards to fall back on in a time of crisis, or to qualify for loans on bigger and better homes and cars and more ambitious business ideas, especially when mixed with viable cash flow.

This is the secret that the wealthy know. They build credit cautiously and meticulously, then use it strategically to make the investments they know will pay off for their families for generations.

If you play your cards right, you can access huge amounts of wealth, which you can then invest strategically to gain more wealth, after a few years of meticulous credit building.

Just remember: this is a game of knowledge and skill. If you are not starting off with a huge amount of wealth to fall back on, it is especially important that you study all you can so that you can make the smartest choices and not fall for predatory lenders or scammers who might seek to profit at your expense with bad "investment" opportunities.

Study this game for a few years and you will become a wealth-building expert. I will be here to help you along the way.

CHAPTER 6
WINNING AT CREDIT MIX

BELIEVE IT OR NOT, if you've followed the steps in the previous chapter, you have already won at credit mix! But this is an important part of your credit score, so it's important that you now understand exactly *how* you did that.

"Credit mix" refers to having different types of credit lines that you are successfully paying off each month. Think of it as demonstrating a variety of different skills in the game of credit. If you are a coach recruiting for a team, you want a player who has shown that they can successfully execute many skills and techniques. A player who is very, very good at a wide range of skills will likely be offered a better contract than someone who is very good at just one skill. The same is true when it comes to loans and credit cards.

How do you demonstrate a variety of skills in the game of credit? Well, you do it by paying off credit lines with different sorts of payment terms. Here are some different types of credit accounts you can get to demonstrate that you have a diverse skill set. You may recognize these terms from the previous chapter:

INSTALLMENT LOANS

Installment loans are loans where you pay a fixed amount to a creditor each month. This demonstrates to banks and credit card companies that you are capable of paying significant amounts of money back over a long period of time. It shows that you are able to plan ahead and borrow only what you can pay back, even many months or years in advance.

A history of successfully paying off installment loans shows creditors that it is safe to lend you large amounts of money, because you won't let them down when it comes to repayment.

You may recognize this model from SelfLender.com in the previous chapter. You agreeing to pay a fixed amount to your savings account each month—and then actually doing it—will show credit bureaus that have this skill. Paying off a student loan or other type of loan with installment payments would show them the same thing, but with Self-Lender.com you don't pay interest on the money you "borrowed" and you are not in danger of showing losses on your scorecard if you can't pay.

Still, you are building and demonstrating the same kind of skill set necessary to pay off a student loan, home, car, or business loan. This means that lenders will be more likely to approve you for such loans in the future. The more you can demonstrate this skill through a long credit history or paying off more than one loan each month successfully, the more likely they are to offer you excellent interest rates and loan large amounts.

REVOLVING DEBT

Revolving debt refers to debts that change each month or are flexible. A common example of a revolving debt is a credit card, where you have the freedom to borrow and pay back as little as $0 or as much as thousands of dollars each month.

If loans show lenders that you have the skills of planning ahead and following through on long-term commitments, revolving debt shows lenders that you can be trusted with flexibility and freedom in your borrowing power. It shows that you will not borrow more than you can afford if given a high credit limit, and that if for some reason you *have* to charge a major purchase on a credit card you will reliably pay it back.

For you as a borrower, it's likely that you will benefit from having access to both long-term loans with fixed installment payments and flexible credit lines from which you can borrow a little or a lot each month depending on your needs. Flexible credit lines like credit cards usually don't have high enough limits to be used to buy a house or a new car, but they can be used to pay a few months' expenses in case of emergency or one-time business expenses.

Since you will benefit from access to the best terms and the highest limits on both installment and revolving types of credit accounts, it makes sense to demonstrate both types of skills to credit bureaus and future lenders.

You may recognize the credit card from Credit Builder in the previous chapter as a type of revolving account. This is one of several reasons I recommend that those who are able take advantage of all three resources in that chapter. By doing so, you will not only be winning three different credit games each month; you will be demonstrating both the skills needed to successfully obtain big home and business loans, and low-interest, high-limit credit cards from regular commercial lenders in the future.

OPEN ACCOUNTS

An open credit account is a credit account which allows for flexible spending like a credit card, but which requires the balance to be paid in full each month.

This type of credit line can be considered an expert-level display of skills: since you are not allowed to defer the balance you charge to future months under any circumstances, it really shows your ability to pay things back in a timely fashion.

I have not included suggestions for open account types here

because these are somewhat rare, and can be highly risky since it is easier for financial shortfalls to harm your credit score instead of helping it with this type of account. This type of account is not necessary to build credit rapidly, so I don't necessarily recommend it to my clients on the personal side. Instead, you may be better off simply opening another ordinary credit card once your credit score moves into the "good" range and you can qualify for low interest rates.

But because this is a type of account recognized by credit bureaus as a potential skill demonstrator, I wanted to let you know that these types of accounts exist and can speed up your credit building process if you don't have the kind of financial uncertainty that can lead to a missed payment.

MORTGAGE ACCOUNTS

Mortgage accounts, like open accounts, are an expert-level skill. They are considered separate from other types of loans because they may have special terms such as variable interest rates. The possibility that your interest rates may change in some mortgages, as well as the sheer size of the loan they represent, makes them another expert-level skill.

Like open accounts, I don't recommend that people take on a mortgage just to optimize their credit mix. Mortgages come with a lot of risk of harm to your credit score if you can't pay them, and as with open accounts, you are unlikely to qualify for favorable interest rates until *after* your credit is already good. As we discussed in a previous chapter, a poor interest rate on a mortgage can cost you over $100,000 in payments you could have avoided over time in some cases!

So if you don't already have a mortgage, don't go out and get one just to build your credit score faster. Wait until you have a good credit score that can get you a good interest rate and other favorable terms upfront. But if you do already have a mortgage, know that this is also counting positively toward your credit mix. You are showing real skill by paying that off!

GROWING YOUR CREDIT PORTFOLIO

Starting with RentReporter.com, a Credit Builder Card, a Self-Lender "loan," and Kikoff will put you on the road to growing credit fast by demonstrating multiple wins each month and a diverse mix of skills.

As your skills and your credit history grow, you will want to begin adding additional lines of credit for multiple reasons. These will help you build credit history faster; they will also give you more financial security and allow you to invest in yourself as you obtain low-interest credit cards and loans that can be used to cover emergency expenses, go to school, or start a business.

Just know that, as you do this, you will want to follow a few simple rules for best results:

1. Don't take out loans you don't need. You don't want to spend money you otherwise wouldn't *just* to boost your credit history. Instead, use SelfLender.com to demonstrate your loan skills, and only take out loans when there's something you actually want or need such as a car, degree, home, or business funding.

2. In loans and credit cards, play for the best possible interest rate. The higher your credit score is when you apply for a loan or credit card, the better interest rates and rewards you are likely to be offered. And different credit card companies and lenders will probably offer you different interest rates and repayment terms when the time comes to apply. As we've now seen, poor interest rates can cost you a lot of money with no benefit to yourself.

3. Research at least six competitors *before* you apply. As we mentioned in this chapter, hard inquiries that lenders perform when deciding whether they want to lend to you, and what terms they want to offer, actually harm your credit score. For that reason, compare what different credit card companies and lenders are offering to customers like yourself *before* you apply, so that you can be sure to apply to

only the one or two best options and minimize your hard inquiries. We'll discuss more about how to minimize hard inquiries when applying for loans in the next chapter

Congratulations! You're now all set to begin building your credit history with a robust credit mix, which means faster growth of your credit score. Now we'll discuss how to win in another column of the credit game score card: new credit.

CHAPTER 7
NEW CREDIT

WE MENTIONED EARLIER that coaches may be worried about hiring a player who seems overcommitted. If a player has just recently started playing for three new teams, how can you as a coach know that they will be able to keep up with all of those game schedules? You might also ask whether they're taking on so many contracts because they're struggling to pay their bills.

The same is true when it comes to opening new credit accounts. This is the reason why hard inquiries harm your credit score. Hard inquiries occur when a credit card company or potential lender reports to a credit bureau that you have asked for a new line of credit.

If you only do this once in a while, the benefits of having that new line of credit added to your credit history will probably outweigh the cost of the inquiry; but if you apply to many credit cards or lenders in a short span of time those hard inquiries can harm your credit score in a big way. And here's why.

Applying to many credit cards and lenders may be seen by credit bureaus that you're taking on more debt than you can manage. If you plan to start paying multiple loans and credit card bills at the same time—well, what are the chances that you will be successful in winning so many games for teams you're not used to playing for?

And there's another concern too. *Why* are you applying for all these loans and credit cards? Are you in big financial trouble, which might indicate that you might be less successful at paying all your bills in the future?

The frustrating part of this scoring system is that the number of hard inquiries reported to credit bureaus often doesn't accurately reflect how much money you actually want to borrow.

Having many hard inquiries doesn't necessarily mean that you want to take out six loans, or open six new credit cards; it could just mean that you *applied* to six lenders with a plan to only accept the best offer you got as part of a wise, strategic credit move.

But the credit bureaus don't know your intentions. If they get six hard inquiries, they'll assume you actually wanted all six credit cards. And there's nothing you can do about that, except study and strategize to get the absolute best offers with the absolute minimum number of hard inquiries.

As with all things in the credit game, knowledge is power. If you don't know how hard inquiries work, you can end up severely damaging your credit without even doing anything irresponsible. I have been in this exact position.

When I decided that my credit was good enough to get favorable terms on a car loan, I was so proud of myself. I had worked so hard to build my credit score, and it was about to pay off. I was going to be a responsible borrower: I was going to compare rates from a few different car dealerships to ensure I got the best possible terms and interest rates I could to save the most money.

There was just one problem: I didn't realize that every single dealership I applied with would send several hard inquiries to multiple lenders on my behalf. In effect, it would look to the credit bureaus like I was either unqualified to purchase a vehicle and desperate or trying to take out multiple different car loans at the same time.

Now, instead of just a few hard inquiries hitting my account, there were about 40 of them, all stemming from the three car dealers I had applied to!

My credit score was devastated, all because I decided to be a responsible comparative buyer when seeking a single modest car loan.

It wasn't fair. I didn't ask those dealers to behave that way on my behalf, and they weren't exactly looking out for my best interest by warning me that this would happen. They were only interested in getting the best possible loans *for themselves* on my behalf. I might have decided not to apply with them at all if I knew it would hurt my credit score. Too bad they weren't going to go out of their way to warn me about that either.

This was one of the hard lessons that compelled me to become a credit expert and educator. Studying what had happened in the aftermath, I learned that there was a way I could have gotten all the same comparative buying benefits while putting only *one* hard inquiry on my account. Here's how to do it!

SECURING FINANCING IN ADVANCE

What I didn't know when I applied for financing to all those car dealerships was that I *could* have come to them with financing already in hand. Then they would not have each sent out multiple inquiries on my behalf, and I would have gotten to compare their offers at no cost to myself.

How could I have done this? I could have gotten approved for a car loan through my bank or any other auto loan company or lender before I ever went to the dealerships.

If you have a bank account, you already have a relationship with a financial institution that may be willing to offer financing on items like car and business loans. Like all creditors, they will take your credit history into account: the better your score already is when you apply, the more favorable the terms you will get. But since they're the ones who get to hang onto your money in the bank, they may have more incentive to lend to you than a random lender would.

In fact, that in itself is a fact that few people know about banks. Banks are allowed to use the money you have sitting in your account to make investments of their own as long as they pay you back with interest. This, in fact, is *why* your savings account accrues interest over time; by having money sitting in your bank account, you are effectively lending your bank money that your bank can now invest in making profit for itself.

Now, don't run and take your money out of the bank! Those interest payments you receive from your bank are a good thing. But you may wish to consider shopping around for the bank or credit union in your area that offers you the best interest rate payments on that money, or the one whose investments are most in line with your ethics and values.

Either way, now that you know that banks profit off of the money in your account, you understand why your own bank or credit union may have more incentive to offer you a better financing deal than a stranger who doesn't get to invest the money in your bank account, but only the money it can *extract* from your bank account.

And now you know that, in some cases, you can win the credit game by securing funding from your bank or credit union in advance instead of applying through multiple companies for financing.

ASKING THE RIGHT QUESTIONS

You can save yourself from a lot of hard inquiries if you ask the right questions when seeking a loan or a credit line. For example, would you have known before reading this book to look for lenders that don't send hard inquiries to credit bureaus at all, like Credit Builder Card or Self Lender? Would you have known that there was a way you could compare deals across multiple car dealerships with just one hard inquiry on your credit file?

When seeking a new loan or credit card, you can ask questions like:

- Will there be a hard inquiry on my account because of this? Will there be more than one?
- How can we minimize the number of hard inquiries on my account? Lenders and credit card companies just want to get

paid, so they may be able to offer ways to get the same amount of financing with fewer hard inquiries.

- What do you think are the best terms you can offer me? If companies know you will only put in a serious application with the company that offers you the best terms, they will probably be happy to tell you about the best deals they have to offer you to try to coax you into applying with them.

With these tools under your belt, you can optimize your credit history and make the most of every dollar you earn to invest in your future.

CHAPTER 8
GETTING TO "PAID AS AGREED"

"Paid as agreed" is the touchdown of the credit world. It is the best possible payment status that you want all of your accounts to show every single month.

The easiest way to do that is to pay all your bills in full and on time. But we all know that isn't always possible. Surprise expenses and shortfalls happen. In some cases, creditors can even fail to notify us that we owe them money while marking us down as non-paying. As long as you are meeting the monthly minimum required payment on all accounts you are paying as agreed, but be careful on accruing interest.

The good news is, it is possible to get your account to "paid as agreed" even long after the original due date has passed. Like the other matters discussed in this book you just have to know *how*.

Some creditors and even debt collectors will change the status of a long past-due account to "paid as agreed" in exchange for full payment. This is the incentive they hold out to you to pay them. You may already have a derogatory mark on your credit report because your bill to them is overdue, but you can have that negative mark erased as though it never happened if you pay the bill now.

However, not all creditors do this automatically. This means that you will want to reach a clear understanding with your creditor that your account status will be changed to "paid as agreed" when you have paid off your balance. This is the only way to ensure that this loss on your scorecard has the best chance of being removed.

So how do you reach such an agreement?

GET IT IN WRITING

Any agreement you reach with *anyone* in your life involving finances should be documented in writing. This allows a court to see clear physical evidence that both parties agreed to these terms, and that you are owed what you were promised for completing your side of the deal.

It is also a good idea to communicate with anyone you might have a complaint with in life such as an employer, doctor, or family member in writing so that there is physical evidence of any problem they have caused you, and of the fact that you let them know about this problem and asked them to help you solve it at the time. That has nothing to do with credit—it's just good to know.

If things go poorly, being able to present a written, signed and time stamped document showing what happened and how both parties agreed to solve the situation is the best way to ensure that justice is done. Any verbal agreement, such as an agreement made via phone call or in-person conversation, is harder to enforce in court since the different parties can give different accounts of what happened. Getting something in writing leaves no doubt.

In the modern world, the easiest way to get an agreement in writing is via email. Email has the added bonus of recording not only the contents of your conversation, but the exact time and date at which the conversation took place and the exact email address of the person you are having the conversation with. That makes it easy to prove who said what and when.

When having a conversation with a creditor about paying a bill where late payment or nonpayment has harmed your credit score, ask for an email or letter stating in writing that they will report the account status to the credit bureaus as "paid as agreed" upon receipt of the payment. If they refuse, you will have less to gain by paying them—and they know that.

During this conversation, you will also want to ask for the best email address to send an email to yourself if the requested email does not show up in your inbox. It is easiest to write an email in reply to an email you've already received, after all, so this will help you make it easier for the creditor to write you this email if they have trouble.

How might you go about asking for something like this? Below I'll share phone and email scripts you can use to help get all of your accounts to "paid as agreed."

PHONE SCRIPT

Many creditors and debt collectors will contact you via phone call, or ask you to call their number as their first line of communication. This is because it's harder to ignore a phone call than an email, and people are more likely to reach a decision to pay if they are encouraged to do so in real-time. Here is a phone script to use when speaking with a creditor or debt collector about getting your account to "paid as agreed."

HOW TO NEGOTIATE WITH BILL COLLECTORS

Remember, you will want to check how close your debt is to expiring under the seven-year statutory limit before contacting any creditor. When you contact them to pay, the clock will reset to "zero" and the derogatory mark will now remain on your credit report for seven years from the date you contact them. So if the bill is already five or six years old, you may not wish to re-start this clock.

For debts which are less than five years old, you may wish to expedite a faster removal from your credit report. In the event that you choose to contact a creditor to arrange this, here are instructions you can use to improve the results of your conversations with this creditor.

Always ask and record who you are talking to. Under the Fair Debt

Collection Practices Act, collectors must identify themselves and the company they work for. If a debt collector or other creditor volunteers this information; write it down. If they don't, ask for the information and then write it down.

Write down the exact date and time of your phone conversation, and its contents. This information may help you later if a dispute arises. If helpful, you may wish to email this information to yourself so that there will be a record on your email server.

"What is your name and the company you work for?"

Immediately write this information down, alongside the date and time of the conversation, when you receive it. You will want to take notes on everything the creditor says during your conversation, ideally writing or typing these notes as you are speaking to them.

Next, tell the creditor your situation.

"I am in a difficult financial position and am behind on my payments. My account number is ____. I'd like to catch up. What kind of payment plan can we arrange?"

You *don't* have to agree to what the creditor proposes. Instead, listen to see what they offer, and see if it is something you can afford. Never agree to borrow money from others, refinance your home, or put debt in a credit card to pay a debt.

If there is no way you can afford to pay under the terms the creditor requests, you may wish to work with a debt settlement lawyer or other financial expert to pursue a more favorable arrangement. If the creditor suggests that you pay more than you can afford, tell them the amount that you have in your budget to pay them.

"I am currently working with a professional with my financial situation. I can pay your company______________ per month for the next _______ months."

Creditors will want to obtain as much payment from you as they can. But if they think the alternative is receiving nothing, they may agree to a more modest payment plan, or even to accept less than the full amount of the debt.

If they offer to accept less than the full amount of the debt or you intend to ask for this, make sure to stipulate that you will need the creditor to agree in writing to report your status as "BIF"—"Balance in Full"—to the credit bureaus. This status looks much better to bureaus than "SIF," which stands for "Settled in Full."

"Once I've made the payments we've agreed upon, we agree that any derogatory information about this account will be removed from my credit report, and my status will be reported to all three credit bureaus as Balance in Full."

Ask what the best email address is to contact the company for a written agreement to report you as BIF once you have paid them the agreed-upon amount.

Once you have obtained an email address or snail mail address, send a confirmation letter to confirm in writing what was discussed today. The notes you have been taking in your phone call log will come in handy for this purpose.

If you send a snail mail letter, keep a copy of the letter and a record of the date and time at which you sent it.

"Thank you <name of collector> of <name of their company>, for working with me.

We agree that I will make monthly payments of _____ beginning on <date> for a total payoff amount of $______________. In return, my status will be reported to all three credit bureaus as "Balance in Full." This letter is to confirm the conclusions of our phone conversation from <date and time of conversation>.

Since we have now reached an agreement, please remove me from your call list. For our mutual protection, we should communicate in writing only from this point on. I do not want you to call me again.

Thank you again for understanding my situation. I am glad we could reach a mutually agreeable arrangement."

If you cannot reach an arrangement that you can afford or which you wish to enter into with the debt collector, tell them you do not wish to pay this debt. This may result in the debt remaining on your credit report for another seven years, but you can stop harassment from debt collectors in this way. If they contact you again after you've told them you do not wish to pay, they've likely violated a law.

Here is a script you can use when requesting no further contacts:

"Please give me the address or email address to which I should send a refusal to pay and cease and desist letter in accordance with the law. I am revoking permission for you to call me at any phone number. I am making a written record of this revocation of permission."

NEGOTIATING TO PAY LESS

It is sometimes possible to negotiate with creditors to pay less than the full amount they are asking for while still getting to "paid as agreed" status. However, this must be done within a certain time window, and requires the use of very specific wording and some knowledge of the collections industry to be successful.

Because the way to do this successfully is not simple, may be different depending on the type of creditor, and is not possible for accounts whose time window has passed, I have not attempted to address every possible situation that may arise here. However, I do offer assistance with these techniques as part of my Major League Credit Repair services.

I also offer you the following template for a letter (not a phone call —you need this in writing!) for your use if you wish to try this technique without assistance:

To Whom It May Concern:

On (Date), I received a copy of my credit report from (Credit Bureau Name). That report lists my payments to you as being 'delinquent.'

My financial problems are now behind me and I am in a position to pay off this debt. I can pay a lump sum amount of $______ or I can pay installments in the amount of $______ per month for ______ months if you will agree to one of the following:

( ) If I make a lump sum payment, you will agree to remove all negative information from my credit file associated with the debt.

( ) If I agree to pay off the debt in monthly installments, you agree to 're-age' my account - making the current month the first repayment month and showing no late payments as long as I make the agreed upon monthly payments.

If this offer is acceptable to you, please check and initial one of the above choices, sign your acceptance below and return this letter to me in the enclosed envelope.

Thank you for your time and assistance.

Sincerely yours,

Unfortunately, this script may have lower chances of success if used without assistance. It may not be possible to negotiate at all if the time window for doing so on a specific debt has passed, and as with all negotiations, there is an art to determining what offer will be appealing enough to be accepted while still being optimally beneficial to you. This is where an experienced expert's eye can be useful.

My Major League Credit Repair services also offer assistance with legally complex situations like bankruptcy, identity theft, and other unfortunate circumstances that may occur when bills go unpaid. We have experts including experienced attorneys who are available free of charge to those who have documentation proving negligence or inaccurate reporting of a debt.

I have not attempted to advise about these in this book because they happen to few people and mistakes made in dealing with them can be costly, but if you are experiencing such a situation, don't hesitate to reach out to my Major League Credit Repair company for help!

CHAPTER 9
DISPUTING ERRORS

IN ADDITION to navigating the credit game to win as much as possible, unfortunately, we have to worry about errors on our scorecard. Whether because of bureaucratic errors or identity theft, we can end up with charges and derogatory marks on our credit report for purchases we never made or bills we've already paid.

This is one reason why it's so important to monitor your credit report and credit score: you can do everything right, and it is still possible that your score will take a hit which you will need to work to resolve.

Credit report errors happen often in two basic ways. It's worth taking the time to discuss both of them so that you will be well-equipped to prevent and address them.

IDENTITY THEFT

Identity theft is an increasingly serious problem in the digital age. More and more online transactions means it's easier than ever before for impersonators to steal your credit or identity information, and use that information to make purchases or open lines of credit in your name.

Since these imposters will not take hits to their own credit score as a result of nonpayment, they will have no incentive to pay the bills they rack up while using your identity. You can then be unpleasantly surprised with negative marks on your credit score or calls from creditors and debt collectors.

Avoiding identity theft means keeping your information safe. That means not giving information that can be used to open accounts in your name to people you don't know well (or to *anybody* else if you can help it), and being cautious when transmitting such data on the Internet.

Pieces of information that can potentially be used by a stranger to open a credit account in your name include:

- Your full legal name
- Your date of birth
- Your phone number
- Your Social Security Number
- Any information about your past or current street addresses
- Any information about your past or current loan history
- Information about your pets, your mother's maiden name, or other questions that may be used as security questions for your online accounts.

Because of these risks, be cautious of any individual or website that asks for such information. Is it a trusted website that you are engaging with for purposes of conducting business, such as the website of a credit bureau or your existing bank or creditor?

The same goes for unsolicited phone calls. Never give any of this information on the phone to a stranger who calls your telephone. If someone calls claiming to be from a company you do business with and asks for this information, it's a good idea to hang up and call the trusted phone number you have for that company to ask whether the call was legitimate. In this way you may protect not only yourself, but also protect others by helping the company become aware of scammers who are impersonating them.

Some organizations which are impersonated by scammers hoping to extract money or information that can be used to steal your identity include:

- The IRS. (Generally, the IRS will never call you and demand money or your Social Security number. They communicate almost exclusively through postal mail.)
- Credit card companies. (Generally these will not make unsolicited phone calls; you will be the one calling them if you are applying, and they will usually communicate any problems with your account via postal mail or through an online account portal with a secure, verified website you have signed up with.)
- Other government agencies. Some scammers have even called immigrants falsely posing as the government of their home country in an effort to extract money and identity information from them. Talk about underhanded!

The Internet is another important frontier for safety. Most legitimate companies have online portals which may ask for some of the above information to verify it's really you. This is done in order to *prevent* identity theft. But be wary of any website which asks for the information above which you are *not* already doing business with.

The same rules about phone calls apply to unsolicited emails you receive. Legitimate companies generally will not request information such as your Social Security number via email. Some scammers and identity thieves may also send emails posing as an organization you do business with, containing a link to a website that asks you for this information.

If you are not completely positive that an email came from the company you do business with, it's a good idea to call the company and check. Any information a company is asking you to enter into a web form or email, it can usually collect more securely over the phone. You can ask to give them your information via phone instead of through the Internet by calling the business's trusted phone number.

Look the number up yourself from a reliable independent source instead of calling the number listed in a suspicious email or unsolicited phone message to make sure you are getting through to the real organization and not a scammer posing as them.

Unfamiliar websites should never ask for your Social Security number, and "harmless" questions in online quizzes about matters like your childhood pet or the street you grew up on can sometimes be masks for the collection of data to be used in identity theft.

If a website asks for any of this information and you are not sure about its security, it is a good idea to use a search engine to research the organization for any reports of scams, or to call the organization on the phone if you know the company is legit but are not sure that this website is secure.

Arguably one of the most important ways to prevent identity theft in the modern era is simply to avoid transmitting data over public wifi networks.

These are the kinds of networks you run into at airports, coffee shops, and other public spaces. They are accessed by many people, and may appear free to access without the necessity for a password.

The problem is, this freedom of access makes it easier for hackers to steal your data from them. Hackers may even set up their own wireless networks in public spaces which *look* like they are being offered by a local organization, but which may actually be run by an individual who harvests all the data transmitted over the network.

One of the best identity defenses out there is a VPN—a virtual private network which masks and encrypts your data. These are often very affordable, and are growing increasingly popular as they offer many benefits including enhanced privacy and security, and other features.

Another useful tool is your phone's wifi hotspot. A growing number of smartphones have the ability to create their own wireless Internet connection which your computer can use anywhere your phone is present. These wifi hotspots have the same level of security as your cell phone data network, making them safer to use to transmit sensitive data than unsecured networks in public spaces.

Using a phone's wifi hotspot to surf the Internet may eat into your phone's data plan, but when you must transmit data that could be used to commit identity theft in a public place, it's worth the cost in data.

SIMILAR NAME ERRORS

Another common cause of credit report errors is quite simply when two people have similar names. This is more likely when you have a Junior and a Senior in the same family who have the same first and last name, or when you have a very common name like John Smith. In these cases, credit bureaus and creditors alike may get confused and put charges or late payments on the wrong John Smith's account.

Unfortunately this is difficult to avoid, since you don't generally choose your own name at birth. But it may be a factor to consider when considering whether to give a baby exactly the same first and last name as another living person. Most John Smiths will be fortunate enough to get through life without such an error, but if it does happen it can be a real headache to resolve.

DISPUTING ERRORS

If you notice an error on a bill or on your credit report, you will have to dispute it. Today, most companies, including credit bureaus, have a simple button you can press to report a fraudulent charge or dispute an item on your credit report. This is a good first step. However, unfortunately this does not always solve the problem.

When a company rejects your claim of a fraudulent charge or an error on your credit report, you will likely have to resort to sending a lengthy campaign of letters using specific language and dispute tactics to try to get the item removed.

You send letters because you want all of this in writing so that the courts can see that this is a mistake and you have been trying to resolve it; you use specific credit compliance language so that the e-Oscar system can work to your benefit and creditors you are disputing will know that you are aware of the legal remedies available to you if they genuinely have made a mistake and they fail to correct it. Knowing that you are aware that you may be able to sue them over such a mistake gives them incentive to investigate and correct the error.

I am including below a sample of a dispute letter you may wish to send to a credit bureau if you discover an error on your report and the initial dispute you file through their "dispute" function is rejected.

To Whom It May Concern:

I received a copy of my credit report and found the following item(s) to be errors.

{dispute_item_and_explanation}

By the provisions of the Fair Credit Reporting Act, I demand that these items be investigated and removed from my report. It is my understanding that you will re-check these items with the creditor who has posted them. Please remove any information that the creditor cannot verify. I understand that under 15 U.S.C. Sec. 1681i(a), you must complete this reinvestigation within 30 days of receipt of this letter.

Sincerely yours,

If you do not receive a satisfactory response within 60 days of sending this letter, here is another letter you can send to escalate the situation:

To Whom It May Concern,

This letter is a formal complaint that you are reporting inaccurate and incomplete credit information.

I am distressed that you have included the information below in my credit profile and that you have failed to maintain reasonable procedures in your operations to assure maximum possible accuracy in the credit reports you publish. Credit reporting laws ensure that bureaus report only 100% accurate credit information.

Every step must be taken to assure the information reported is completely accurate and correct. The following information, therefore, needs to be re-investigated. I respectfully request to be provided proof of this alleged item, specifically the contract, note or other instrument bearing my signature.

{dispute_item_and_explanation}

Failing that, the item must be deleted from the report as soon as possible. The listed item is entirely inaccurate and incomplete, and as such represents a very serious error in your reporting. Please delete this misleading information and supply a corrected credit profile to all creditors who have received a copy within the last six months, or the last two years for employment purposes.

Additionally, please provide the name, address, and telephone number of each credit grantor or other subscribers.

Under federal law, you have thirty (30) days to complete your re-investigation. Be advised that the description of the procedure used to determine the accuracy and completeness of the information is hereby requested as well, to be provided within fifteen (15) days of the completion of your re-investigation

Sincerely yours,

This is just one sample—if they do not respond to this letter favorably, you may need to write a series of letters using escalating legal language to resolve the issue. This is another expert-level matter where specific details about what has happened may affect what language you must use in your letter to be successful.

It may also become necessary to provide the credit bureaus with proof that you have done all that is necessary to address the situation on your end, such as supplying proof that you have filed police reports and complaints to the Federal Trade Commission about the theft of your identity.

Because of the complexity of escalating disputes, I am not including further dispute letter templates here. But I do offer a collection of dispute letter templates for a variety of possible situations, and expert advice to help you determine which one is appropriate for your situation through Major League Credit Repair.

Fixing errors on your credit report can be difficult, and you may feel powerless if your first few attempts to have an error corrected are rejected or ignored. But you are not powerless! As you can tell by the language of the second letter, there are laws in place requiring credit bureaus to do their job, and procedures that they must follow. This is called the Fair Credit Reporting Act.

As with all things in the credit game, all you need to gain a big advantage is knowledge, and the patience and persistence to follow the necessary steps to accomplish your goals.

When you have those two things, you have power.

CHAPTER 10
IMPROVING YOUR EXISTING ACCOUNTS

You may already have credit cards, or you may start to open a new credit card account or two after raising your credit score using the techniques in this book. Either way, one little-known fact is that you can often get better terms on your credit accounts after your credit score goes up, even if you opened the account when your credit was not quite so excellent.

Credit card companies compete for great credit players. That means that if they see that you're an all-star and you express that you're less than thrilled with the terms of your current account with them, they will often offer you better terms in an attempt to keep you on their team.

In the eyes of credit card companies, getting paid a low interest rate by someone who always pays their bills on time and who may be on their way to being a big spender is better than getting paid no interest because you left their company and accepted a better offer.

You can ask for improvements to your credit card accounts like:

- A lower interest rate.
- A higher credit limit.

Remember, you don't want to get a higher credit limit because you want to be able to charge $10,000 on your credit card—that would harm your credit! You want to get a higher limit so that you can have more credit available to you in case an emergency leaves you with no other way to pay for things, and so that you can charge more on your account without going over the 10% limit for ideal credit usage that makes your score look great. 30% is the absolute max in case you have to tend to a larger purchase or emergency.

You might get a $10,000 credit limit and never charge more than $1,000 at once on that card. That's actually ideal. But because your credit limit is so high, you can charge a whole $1,000 on there without taking a big hit to your credit score due to high utilization, and you have a whole $10,000 in credit to fall back on if something really bad happens and there's just no other way to put food on the table for a few months.

And once you've got a great interest rate on that card, anything you charge on it will cost you much less than it would have cost to pay for with a payday loan or a higher-interest card.

Once your credit score has gone up, making you a more desirable player than you were before, here are some telephone scripts you can use to call your credit card company and ask for better terms:

LOWER INTEREST RATE TELEPHONE SCRIPT

YOU: Hello, I'd like to lower the APR on my credit card, please.

CREDIT CARD REP: May I ask why?

YOU: I've been a loyal customer to you for X years. Also, I've paid my bill in full and on time for the past few months/years. I know a few other credit cards offering better rates than what I'm getting right now, and I'd hate for this interest rate to drive me away from your service. What can you do for me?

CREDIT CARD REP: Hmm. Let me check…Ms. Patrick, I just discovered that I am able to lower your rate from 15% to 12%. Will this work?

HIGHER CREDIT LIMIT TELEPHONE SCRIPT

YOU: Hello, I'd like to increase the limit on my credit card, please.

CREDIT CARD REP: May I ask why?

YOU: I've been a loyal customer to you for X years. Also, I've paid my bill in full and on time for the past few months/years. I've been offered cards with higher limits by some of your competitors, and I would hate for a low credit limit to drive me away from your service.

CREDIT CARD REP: Hmm. Let me check…Ms. Patrick, I just discovered that I am able to lower your rate from $5,000 to $10,000. Will this work?

It's common that during uncertain economic times, credit card companies may automatically lower the credit card limits of many users. The companies may become concerned about losing money if many users start using them as an emergency fund and can't pay them back.

This happened at the start of the COVID-19 pandemic, when many credit card companies became concerned that large numbers of their customers may soon face job loss or huge medical bills. To reduce the risk to the company, these credit card companies cut many users' credit limits.

When this happens, it is not because the cardholder has done something wrong—it is a systemic measure taken to reduce risk to the company. The company will usually also offer to increase the users' credit limits again once the crisis has passed and the economy is looking up. If your credit limit was cut by your credit card company in 2020 and you have been faithfully paying your bills for the last few months or years, there is a good chance you can now get your credit limit raised back up to its former glory or beyond with a phone call.

IMPROVING LOANS AND MORTGAGES

Other types of credit lines, such as loans and mortgages, can also be improved from their original terms as you learn more about credit and become more creditworthy. These changes tend to be very complex and require a lot of work, however, since the amounts of these loans are often very large.

A clever refinancing may save your family $100,000 or more if done properly, but this can usually only be done with the help of an expert. When taking an interest in refinancing or getting a loan modification, it is important to have a trusted expert on your side. Some companies can offer refinancing deals and loan modifications that sound great in the advertisement, but which contain hidden details in the fine print that can leave you worse off than you were before in the interest of profiting the company.

When seeking an expert to help you with a refinancing or loan modification, look for an expert who is trusted by people you trust and who has reason to have your best interest in mind. You may be able to accomplish something extraordinary—but like all of life's greatest achievements, you probably will not be able to succeed alone.

CHAPTER 11
INTRODUCTION TO BUSINESS CREDIT

You now know the most fundamental principles of personal credit. This powerful knowledge will help you to build generational wealth and avoid the traps of permanent debt and poverty that too many people fall into. There is still more to learn—now that you know how powerful these principles are, you may desire to study some of the complex topics mentioned here and become a credit educator or financial professional yourself someday.

But believe it or not, we've barely scratched the surface of how credit determines who becomes wealthy and who stays poor.

I mentioned that credit can be used to obtain business loans a few times throughout this book. Business loans and business credit cards carry several wealth-building advantages over personal loans and personal credit cards. This is because business loans and business credit are the real heavy lifters in our economy.

For those who know how, tens or hundreds of thousands of dollars in capital to start a business or invest in real estate can be acquired with no money out-of-pocket and little risk to one's personal and family finances. If you also acquire the business know how to multiply that money—something that is totally achievable without going to business school—you can see how you can rapidly build hundreds or millions of dollars for your family and community.

This process begins with building great personal credit. Just like with personal credit, business creditors and lenders will look at your payment history to determine how much they can safely lend you, at what interest rate, and what kinds of collateral in terms of assets they may require you to put on the line in order to approve your loan. When you are first starting out securing business credit, your personal credit score can be used to determine these factors. This can also be done separate from your personal credit by obtaining credit using your business Employer Identification Number also known as an EIN.

Once you have established the basic forms of business credit, you will want to focus on developing positive payment history for your business. Your business has a separate credit score from your personal credit, and that is how you build it.

This is an incredibly powerful tool. It means that, for example, if your business fails due to unforeseen circumstances, its unpaid bills may not affect your personal credit and your personal ability to get home loans, low interest rates, etc. at all. This powerful separation can also work in reverse: if a personal disaster means that you have to declare personal bankruptcy, your business may still be able to obtain big loans and low interest rates as long as your business has been paying its bills.

Separating your business from your personal credit and finances will require incorporating your business as a separate legal entity from you as an individual. Your business will then receive an Employer Identification Number—the business equivalent of a Social Security Number—and will file separate taxes for you as an individual.

This may sound like a hassle, but it is not as intimidating as it sounds. Anyone can incorporate an LLC and begin applying for business credit cards to begin building business credit.

It's important to incorporate your business for other reasons beyond your business credit score. Corporations may sometimes be eligible for special tax breaks, grants, and other programs that individuals cannot qualify for.

Incorporating limits not only your financial liability for the actions of your business, but also the legal liability. If your business is sued or fined, your personal finances may be protected from the fines or the lawsuit if your business is a separate incorporated entity and you were not personally responsible for any wrongdoing.

All of these are reasons to incorporate your business—a move which will also make your business eligible for the tremendous power of business credit.

The majority of you reading this book probably don't yet own a corporation. You may not be ready to start one, either, if your personal credit score is not yet great and might not get you great rates on business credit cards and business loans.

Major League Credit has a proven system that can help you start or grow your business by establishing business credit and accessing various types of loans and capital. Our business credit-building system also comes with six months of personal credit repair! We want to make it easy for you to kill two birds with one stone, since both processes do take time.

So take some time to nurture your credit, and then keep an eye out for my next book. This book will cover the basics of business credit in the same way I've covered the basics of personal credit here, and will detail some of the things that Major League Credit's business credit experts can help you with.

I wish you wealth and happiness in the years to come. You deserve it.

RESOURCES

- *Welcome to Major League Credit & Lending.* https://majorleaguecr.com/
- *Book a Free Consultation with Major League Credit & Lending.* Calendly. https://calendly.com/majorleaguecreditrepair
- SelfLender. *Welcome to Self Lender.* https://self.inc/refer/16576650
- RentReporters. *Report rent payments, Build your credit score.* (2022, June 8). https://prf.hn/l/6bW31aO
- Credit Builder Card. *It's time to Build your credit.* https://www.creditbuildercard.com/majorleaguecreditrepair.html
- Kikoff Credit Builder | Build Credit Safely & Responsibly. *Build credit with Kikoff.* https://kikoff.com/
- Annual Credit Report.com - Home Page. https://www.annualcreditreport.com/index.action
- SmartCredit. *Credit scores and reports with monitoring.* http://www.smartcredit.com/majorleaguecreditrepair
- IdentityIQ. *3 credit scores, Daily Credit Monitoring & Alerts.* https://www.identityiq.com/get-all-your-reports-now.aspx?offercode=431131QO

- Experian.com. Do more with your FICO® score. all free. https://www.experian.com. 1-888-397-3742
- Equifax.com. Credit Bureau: Check your credit report & credit score. https://www.equifax.com. 1-800-525-6285
- Transunion.com. Credit scores, Credit Reports & Credit Check. https://www.transunion.com. 1-800-680-7289.
- Utica University. Identity Theft Victims' Resources. Resources - identity crimes - center for identity management and information protection (CIMIP) - Utica University. https://www.utica.edu/academic/institutes/cimip/idcrimes/resources.cfm
- *Fair credit reporting act.* (2020, March 4). Federal Trade Commission. Retrieved August 1, 2022, from https://www.ftc.gov/legal-library/browse/statutes/fair-credit-reporting-act
- *Fair debt collection practices act.* (2016, March 23). Federal Trade Commission. Retrieved August 1, 2022, from https://www.ftc.gov/legal-library/browse/rules/fair-debt-collection-practices-act-text
- *Major League Credit Repair.* Facebook. https://www.facebook.com/majorleaguecreditrepair
- *Major League Credit Repair.* Instagram. (@majorleaguecredit) • instagram photos and videos. https://www.instagram.com/majorleaguecredit

THE CREDIT GAME

ENTREPRENEUR SECRETS TO BUILDING BUSINESS CREDIT WITHOUT PERSONAL LIABILITY USING EIN

CHEVON K. PATRICK

FREE GIFT FOR READERS

Or Visit: https://www.bit.ly/TCGgift

INTRODUCTION

"Money is a terrible master but an excellent servant."
— P. T. Barnum

Too many people today believe they can't start a business because they don't have the startup capital. After all, you've got to spend money to make money, right? Renting space, buying equipment, hiring employees, and paying for marketing costs are not things the average citizen thinks they can afford.

I'm here to show you how anyone can start a business with no initial credit checks that result in hard inquiries, no cash flow, and no collateral. These are all qualifying factors that traditional lenders require, and they are the factors that limit most business startups' success. This alternative method of funding will not only help you obtain the capital you need, but will also give you time to improve your personal credit if needed. My previous book, *The Credit Game: Plays We Were Never Taught,* can help you with that as well.

The secret here is that most people who successfully start businesses, no matter how wealthy they are or aren't, don't spend their own money to do it. Instead, they use business credit.

My goal with this book is to empower you to start a business that thrives. If you don't think you have the wealth or skills to start a successful business, we'll change that here. And if you already own a business, but it's struggling financially, we will look at tools and strategies you can use to change that too.

Many of us underestimate the importance of credit. If we were raised with an old-school mindset, we might feel that buying anything on credit is like spending money you don't have. Some of us avoid taking out lines of credit at all for that reason. But the reality is much more complex than that.

Those who read my first book, *The Credit Game: Plays We Were Never Taught*, know that credit scores affect far more than how much we can buy without paying up-front. Having a track record of securing and using personal credit responsibly can mean getting better prices, better interest rates, and more purchasing power.

In fact, the financial system is built to punish those who don't buy on credit: if you have no track record for paying back loans or credit cards, you will be considered a less reliable payer for any purchase or loan you might wish to undertake in the future.

The benefits of good business credit—and the consequences of not having it—are even more severe. Having a poor business credit score can mean paying higher insurance premiums, being denied loans and business credit lines, and getting charged high-interest rates that cost you over time. This can limit your business' ability to grow, and can even shut you out of the best markets entirely. Many major vendors and suppliers will not sell to businesses with poor credit scores at all because they don't want to risk their invoices going unpaid.[1]

So how do you build good business credit? The good news is, it's more about having knowledge than about having wealth. As with personal credit, knowing how business credit scores are calculated and what potential lenders and vendors look for in a business' credit history is more important than how much you spend. When you have this knowledge, you can know exactly what types of credit lines to seek, how to use them strategically, and how to grow your borrowing gradually so that you don't get in over your head with debt on an untested business.

We'll see exactly how the system works in this book, just like we did for personal credit in *The Credit Game: Plays We Were Never Taught*.

Business credit is just as important as personal credit in several ways:

- Businesses generally qualify for bigger loans and lines of credit than individuals. Businesses are assumed to have higher expenses and higher cash flow, so business credit lines can help a business to thrive when personal credit is not enough.
- There are laws in place to protect business owners and their families from catastrophe in the event of a business disaster. If you set your business entity up properly and choose the correct lines of credit, your personal credit score and your family's assets will be protected in the event of business bankruptcy or loss.
- When it comes to big purchases, some vendors and creditors may refuse to do business with you *at all* if your business credit score is poor or non-existent.
- It solves the cash access problem here in America for people who don't qualify for traditional bank loans and funding.

I cannot overstate the importance of building business credit to starting a successful business.

A study by the National Small Business Administration found that 27% of small businesses reported that they were struggling, or were unable to take advantage of opportunities for growth because they could not procure sufficient funding.[2] To ensure you can afford to grow when opportunities for growth present themselves, it's a good idea to start building your business credit *now* with small steps that will build up to credit you can draw on to produce major financing in as little as six months.

The following methods can also help qualify you for other major loans when the time comes.

In this book, we'll learn:

- What paperwork and registrations you will need to ensure your business is set up properly and eligible for the best business credit options.
- How to separate your business finances from your personal finances.
- How to build business credit using your Employer Identification Number instead of your Social Security number, keeping your personal assets and finances safe.
- The pros and cons of different types of business credit, and the types of business credit you must get if you want to have an optimal business credit portfolio.
- How to stack different levels of commercial accounts to avoid being a personal guarantor and to save the grief of multiple hard inquiries.
- How to become double, triple, or even quadruple lendable by applying these strategies to every business you own!

As you read this book, I encourage you to "do your homework" as you go along. We'll discuss quite a few pieces of paperwork you will want to file to set up a business entity that is eligible for a business credit score. This paperwork may get overwhelming if you save it all for the end of the book, but it will be easier to break down if you submit a few pieces of paperwork at the end of each chapter before moving on.

My goal here is to help you get it done, just like I did as a small business owner with limited capital. After discovering how powerful credit could be, I have dedicated nearly the last decade to learning everything I could about business and personal credit so I could help people to realize dreams they may never have been able to finance otherwise.

I invite you to read this book twice. Once all the way through, ensure that you know your big-picture strategy from start to finish; then again, chapter by chapter, as you complete the steps contained in each chapter.

You'll find that each chapter contains a number of specific steps that may take a few weeks or more to complete. Some also specify that you should wait two months before moving on to the next steps. But if you take persistent action, you can obtain at least $50,000 in six to twelve months, and maybe even sooner.

This may seem like a long period of time now, but when you have the capital you need to start or grow your business, you'll be glad and wish you started sooner. During this time period of building, your credit history will grow as you apply to creditors, and as reports of bills you have successfully paid on time register with the credit bureaus. Once your business credit has enough positive accounts reporting, it will be healthy and robust enough to take the next big steps.

If you complete all the steps contained in this book within six months or so, you will be in a position to successfully acquire capital and other forms of alternative credit and financing, even if you started out with no money and no business credit score.

You *can* finance your dream. You've just got to know how.

CHAPTER 1
YOUR BUSINESS CREDIT STRATEGY

This book is designed to guide you through the stages of building business credit without having cash flow, collateral, or great personal credit. The term "stages" here is important because, as with any career path, you've got to have a strategy.

Many publicly available sources of information on business credit do not fully explain that some types are riskier or more difficult to get than others, or that having certain types of credit lines in place *before* applying for others can qualify you for more funding and more favorable interest rates without being a personal guarantor.

The widespread lack of cash access and attention to strategy in online how-tos is one reason why so many business owners become frustrated after, for example, applying for a business loan and being rejected. Often, they have never been told that bank loans are one of the most advanced forms of obtaining business capital and that it's a good idea to build their business credit through other methods *before* applying if they want to be approved.

I will begin this book with the assumption that you have no business credit score. You may not yet have taken a single step toward making your business a reality, or you may be a long-time business owner who has been running your business out of your personal wallet because you weren't comfortable applying for business credit or loans.

In either case, we will move from the assumption that you have no business credit score to a position where you can realistically apply for and receive tens or hundreds of thousands of dollars in funding to grow your business at favorable interest rates. This can all be done without risk to your personal credit or assets using a system that worked for me as a first-time business owner.

I will warn you: there will be a lot of paperwork and a little bit of footwork. But as you complete every step in this strategy, you will see how you are establishing your business as a reputable legal entity with a solid financial track record that makes you an appealing client for a bank loan, business grant, and other sources of funding that can stretch well up into the six-figure range.

Let's take a moment to learn about some of the concerns you as a business owner need to be aware of when considering applying for financing. We'll cover some of the risks and trade-offs contained within different types of credit lines, and see why some types of business credit can be riskier for business owners than others.

Meet the Credit Bureaus

The arbiters of credit scores are a group of organizations called credit bureaus. These are private companies, but their jobs are considered so important that they are subject to regulations by the federal government to ensure that they do their jobs thoroughly and fairly. What exactly is the job of credit bureaus? It's to keep track of the "credit scores" of businesses and individuals.

Credit scores are designed to predict the future cash flow of businesses and individuals. This information is then used by vendors, credit card companies, banks, and other entities to decide how much money to lend an individual or business, how much interest to charge, and sometimes whether to do business with a company at all or whether the company seems too distressed or risky.

Because so many potential lenders and business partners will look at our credit scores to make important decisions about our businesses , it's important to understand who the major credit bureaus are and how to make sure the credit reports they put together about our businesses look great. Meet the most important business credit bureaus in the U.S.:

- Dun & Bradstreet. This is the "gold standard" of business credit bureaus by many people because it offers reports, not just on a business's credit history , but also on matters like its "business family tree," which shows a list of businesses with which a given business is legally or financially intertwined.
- Dun & Bradstreet is even experimenting with offering cybersecurity ratings to evaluate a company's risk of suffering a hack or other IT system failure. We will show you how to apply for a D-U-N-S
- number and establish your Dun & Bradstreet credit report in Chapter 2. Equifax business credit scores. Equifax is one of the
- Big 3 credit bureaus which compiles personal credit scores, and they offer business credit scores too. As in personal credit, Equifax is considered one of the most reputable and comprehensive business credit scoring agencies. Experian business credit scores. Like Equifax,
- Experian is considered one of the Big 3 players in both personal and business credit reporting.

Throughout this book, we'll learn how to use our knowledge of these bureaus to build business credit history to the point where we can obtain tens of thousands of dollars in business financing within six months!

DEBT VS. EQUITY

Capital moves in our economy in two forms: debt and equity. "Debt" is when you owe someone something which you are expected to repay later or face adverse consequences. "Equity" is the valuation of ownership, where someone has actually used their infusion of capital to purchase something, like ownership of your company or your assets.

Debt is the most commonly discussed form of capital in credit discussions, as it is generally the way that credit cards, loans, and other common types of credit lines function. However, investors and certain types of "secured" financing will actually trade money for ownership of your business or assets which they can take or sell or make legal decisions for if they so desire.

This is important because giving up equity means giving up...

CONTROL

One major reason people start their own businesses is a desire for control over their craft or their career. While some people start businesses with the specific intention of selling them to a wealthy buyer after the business has become profitable, most entrepreneurs want to be able to run their business their way for some time.

Having all the control means that you also have all the financial responsibility. If you give up some of that financial responsibility, such as by bringing on investors or taking out credit lines that are secured with your assets, you are giving up control. Anyone to whom you give equity in return for capital can have a say in how your business is run.

Even some bank loans may come with requirements that the

bank be allowed to review your business's financial performance and require changes as a condition of obtaining the loan. This is generally not a bad thing as the bank's only interest when lending money is the profitability of your business, and that's your interest too. Banks generally will not try to micromanage your business because their only concern is that you pay them back with interest.

Investors, on the other hand, are less restrained in what they can require of your business. This is why obtaining investors is generally recommended as the *last* step in your business financing journey, and some business owners choose to forego investors altogether.

SECURITY

Credit lines come in both "secured" and "unsecured" varieties. "Secured" lines of credit are those in which your lender "secures" their loan by having you sign legal paperwork stating that you will forfeit certain assets to them, or that they will be able to take certain types of action against you if you don't pay them back.

Be sure you understand what you are signing up to forfeit if you choose to pursue secured lines of credit. Are you willing to lose whatever you are promising if you can't pay this credit line back?

Secured credit lines can have advantages over some unsecured credit lines, such as sometimes having lower interest rates (the lenders' logic is that since they cannot really force borrowers to pay them back, they will charge all of their borrowers' higher interest rates to make up for the money they might lose from some through nonpayment). But there may be times when unsecured lines are better.

You may be beginning to see more examples of why it is so important to understand business credit strategy. New business owners who take on investors without realizing they are losing some control of their business, or who offer their home as an asset to secure a loan may find themselves in very unwelcome territory if their investor starts demanding changes to their business or they encounter problems paying off their secured loan.

TRANSFERABILITY & SEPARABILITY

Two big reasons to build business credit are separability and transferability. Both refer to the question of whether the capital or debt you obtain is yours personally, or belongs to your business.

For business reasons, it may be desirable to be able to transfer your business's financial assets, such as its credit history and its capital, to other owners. This may be useful, for example, if you decide to sell your business to a new business owner for a large lump sum of money when you retire, or if you have a business partner to whom you want to be able to transfer some financial duties.

It is also highly desirable to maintain your business capital and debts separate from your personal assets and your personal credit score. New businesses are inherently risky and ensuring that debts stay with your business, not with your personal credit score or your personal assets, means that you can protect assets like your home and credit score even if the worst happens to your business.

Generally, transferability and separability go together: if debts and capital are linked to your business as a separate legal entity, not to you personally, then you have the power to transfer them to future owners of your business.

EASE OF ATTAINMENT

Some types of credit are more readily given out than others. This may be because they are only small loans or credit lines and do not represent a large risk to the lender, or it may be because the consequences for failing to pay them back are so severe that the lenders have a high confidence that they will be paid back.

Both in personal finance and business, it's important to understand *why* it is easy to obtain any line of credit you are offered. Is it because it's a mutually beneficial situation for you and the lender? Or because the lender knows they will extract far more money from you in repayment than you are actually borrowing?

In my simple business credit-building strategy, we will focus first on lines of credit that are both low-risk and easy to obtain. This will allow you to start building credit history with relatively low risk. We will then move on to more exclusive and more challenging types of credit, allowing you to build your skills over the course of six months or so. This can be thought of as the fastest possible timeline for building your skills and credit using an optimal strategy within the confines of the business credit system.

In the four tiers I use to discuss business finances, lower-tier types of financing are generally those which are lower-risk and easier to obtain, while higher-tier types are either riskier or harder to obtain. The presumption is that as business owners master less risky types of credit and build credit history, they will develop the credit history and the skills they need to obtain and successfully profit from more challenging types of financing.

It's worth noting that the phrase "tiers" may be used in different ways by different parties in the credit and finance world. Experian, for example, uses "Tier 1 credit" to refer to the very *best* business credit which is accomplished through many years of work.[1]

I don't find this approach useful since it does not help business owners to build their credit step-by-step from the ground up, and specific credit score numbers can be used to more precisely understand one's chances of approval for new lines of credit. So in this book when we refer to "tiers" of business credit, we will also be referencing the following terms:

PERSONAL GUARANTOR

Most business owners know nothing about business credit and often use their personal credit to start or grow their business. Unfortunately, about 29% of businesses fail and end up costing business owners their personal assets, savings accounts, and personal investments in the process.

This book teaches an alternative way to master business credit so that it does not hold you, the business owner, personally liable for the business's debts and commitments. "No personal guarantee" means not risking your home or your vehicle, or having to mix finances.

Opting out of being a guarantor will also protect you from losing credit score points caused by multiple hard inquiries when applying for business credit lines, for example. This means you can continue to enjoy excellent personal credit and all the perks that come with it even as you rapidly open new lines of credit for your business.

TIER 1: NET TERM VENDOR ACCOUNTS

Nearly all businesses that buy supplies from vendors have some sort of basic trade credit. These are credit lines where vendors and suppliers agree to allow businesses to purchase supplies and equipment on credit and pay them back over time. These can include vendor credit, retail credit, and equipment leases that usually come with a net 10, net 15, net 30, or net 60 trade account.

"Net" here means the full amount of your invoice is due within the number of days specified. Net 10 or net 15 accounts must be paid off in as little as 10-15 days after your purchase or when the invoice is sent out, while net 30s or net 60s may afford more time.

To start building your business credit, I recommend using net 30 accounts. This is because these accounts offer a good balance of time and speed. Also note that in order to activate the

majority of these accounts, a purchase anywhere between \$50-
\$100 must be made for it to report to the bureaus.

Typically, payments are collected and reported to the credit
bureaus every 30 days, which allows you to build up multiple
positive payment reports from several vendors in just one
month. But because net 30 accounts give you a full month to pay,
the chances of you forgetting or being unable to pay are lower
than if you were trying to pay off your accounts every 10 or 15
days. Remember, what you *don't* want to do is take out a line of
credit and then forget to pay it back by the deadline!

Net 30 accounts are usually offered by vendors who sell
specific business supplies. The highly specific nature of these
credit lines makes them both easy to obtain and low risk. The
vendor or supplier knows that you can only use their line of
credit to buy from them, so you aren't going to go out and use
the credit line they've given you on something else and subsequently fail to pay it back.

If you successfully use their supplies to make a profit and
pay them back, you're extremely likely to continue buying from
them in the future, so they will have gained a long-term
customer. If you fail to pay them back, they can stop supplying
you or repossess their equipment and take a relatively small loss.

This means that offering these trade credit lines is a good
investment for the vendors and suppliers who offer them, so
they are more eager to offer them to new businesses with little
credit history than someone might be to offer a credit line that is
higher-risk and less profitable to the lender like a credit card or a
loan.

TIER 2: ADVANCED TRADE CREDIT

More advanced levels of trade or vendor credit are best for businesses that have spent a couple of months building up a solid
history of successfully paying off their tier 1 net accounts. These
advanced credit lines may allow you to borrow larger amounts
and take more time to pay them back than with basic trade credit

lines. They may also allow you to buy a broader range of products and look more impressive to potential business partners and creditors in your credit report.

That's good for your business if you are looking to expand and you want the ability to buy more supplies or equipment and pay for these items after you've expanded your operation and are profiting from them. But it can also be risky because if for some reason, you *don't* profit from the new purchases, you can be stuck, unable to pay the lender back a larger amount of money. In that case, both you and the lender face negative consequences.

You must not miss or have any late payments on these accounts, because building credit in this manner is solely based on payment history. This fact makes business credit much more unforgiving of these types of mistakes.

That's why these more flexible and expansive lines of trade credit are considered "Tier 2": they're best for businesses who have already learned to reliably turn supplies and equipment into profit by using basic trade credit lines for at least two months.

You may also be introduced to fleet credit in this tier. Fleet credit is used by companies like Amazon that have a fleet of vehicles. Although you don't have to have a "fleet" of vehicles, this type of credit line allows the ability to manage fuel costs and save on expenses such as vehicle maintenance.

TIER 3: REVOLVING CREDIT

As you continue to build your business credit history, you will apply for more challenging and more flexible lines of business credit after each milestone. Now that you have proven your ability to pay back your debts thoroughly using net-term accounts, it's time to look into tradelines that require more trust and offer more power.

Lenders may now be willing to offer you revolving lines of credit which do not require payment in full each month. For the purposes of our strategy, we are still using these tradelines primarily to maximize your business credit history so that you will become eligible for even bigger and better financing opportunities in the future. This means being conservative with their use, since having an impeccable payment history is vital to getting to the truly top tier of business credit and financing.

But this is also the point at which your new business credit lines can save you some serious cash on your business expenses, and allow you to do things you probably could not have done using personal credit alone. For this reason, it may be worth investigating which credit lines offer the best rewards programs and discounts for your business model, and considering that separately from the question of whether they report rapidly to the most desirable credit bureaus.

If you follow my directions, you will get to the point where you begin to become approved for these higher-end credit options within four months.

TIER 4: HIGH-LIMIT REVOLVING CREDIT

The last credit tier we'll discuss in this book will be high-limit and cash lines of credit. These are the biggest, most powerful, and most difficult to obtain business credit lines. They can include business credit cards with very high credit limits and very favorable interest rates and rewards programs, and other types of financing you may not have heard about before.

The risk-benefit trade-off here is obvious. A skilled business owner can do a *lot* with these lines of credit, and they show banks, investors, and other potential lenders or business partners that you are very good at managing your finances. But they also carry a high potential for both you and the lender to get into serious financial difficulty if you are given one of these highly flexible, high-limit credit lines, and you spend money on things you aren't able to turn into profit.

Whether and when to apply for these credit lines will be up to you. My job here is to help you build the business credit score that will make this an option for you and to give you a chance to learn exactly how to turn credit into profit within your chosen business model as you learn to use safer and more modest credit lines along the way.

OUR 5-STEP BUSINESS CREDIT BUILDING SYSTEM

In this book, we will progress through the following steps:

1. Building your foundation by filing the appropriate legal documents to establish your business as a legal entity with finances separate from your own and which is eligible for its own credit rating.
2. Optimizing your business's financial profile to demonstrate to lenders that your business and its owner are reliable borrowers who will yield profit in the form of interest payments for anyone who lends to them.
3. Create and optimize profiles with the business credit reporting agencies, whose reports are used by lenders to decide whether to lend to a business.
4. Start vendor credit. This is a basic type of business credit that is often available with favorable terms relative to all-purpose credit lines. This will begin establishing your business's credit history as a reliable borrower with favorable payment terms.
5. Start revolving credit lines. This is another type of specialized business credit line that is broader in applicability and sometimes more challenging to manage. This makes it an excellent demonstration for future lenders that your business can handle multiple types of credit lines reliably.
6. If desired, at this stage you can also begin building cash credit by taking out more all-purpose business credit lines such as business credit cards. These can be useful to your business, but can also be more

challenging to manage because they have fewer restrictions and can be easier to overspend on. For this reason, I only recommend this strategy for those with healthy spending habits and a solid business plan.

So how can you take your business from concept to major financial player? Let's get started by procuring everything you'll need to obtain at least five to six basic trade credit lines!

CHAPTER 2
BUILD YOUR FOUNDATION

Starting a business can be intimidating, even if you're not thinking about credit and funding. The necessary legal and financial steps will vary depending on a business's industry, the city and state it operates in, and who runs it. Although some businesses can get away with far less paperwork than others, having specific pieces of legal paperwork in place makes it possible to build business credit which is separate from your personal credit and finances, not to mention making it easier to handle issues like legal liability and taxes.

A new business may need to:

- Legally register with their city, state, and local governments.
- Register as a legal entity such as a Limited Liability Corporation or an S-Corporation.
- Pay sales tax and/or business income tax.
- Create a business bank account.
- Apply for business loans or credit lines.
- Hire subcontractors or employees.
- Make legal and financial arrangements with suppliers, vendors, and partner businesses.

- Be prepared to deal with potential customer, employee, or subcontractor lawsuits.

This list deters many people from starting their own businesses, as many of these steps sound difficult or complicated. However, here I will show that they're not hard to do. We will go through the major steps necessary to set a business up for legal or financial success together.

I need to put a major disclaimer here: because laws vary by city and state, you should *also* consult your city and state's laws on these matters. I will share general information from a U.S. federal perspective, but the regulations for your city or industry may differ. Some states require more paperwork, licenses, and fees than others, and the same business may or may not need a license, depending on the city and state it is located in.

My goal here is to give you a good start so that by the time you go through these steps, performing any additional steps your city or state may require of you will seem easy!

HOW AND WHY SHOULD YOU REGISTER YOUR BUSINESS?

Registering a business means filing paperwork with your city and state to establish your business as an official legal entity. This is usually required in order to file taxes and procure business credit, as lenders and creditors need legal documentation proving that a business is an established legal entity before they can start reporting its credit score to credit bureaus and certainly before they will think about lending a business money.

Incorporating your business as a legal entity can also offer some protection against the consequences of bankruptcy and lawsuits, since these may be filed against the *business* as a legal entity instead of against the owners as individuals.

This is not a "get out of jail free" card—if a business owner can be proven personally responsible for legal or financial misconduct, they may still be the recipient of the consequences. But under other circumstances, the owner can be partially shielded from the consequences of circumstances beyond their control. This is especially true if the business owner purchases industry-appropriate liability insurance, which usually also requires that the business be legally registered in order for the insurance to be properly applied.

So what is the first step to registering your business?

NAMING YOUR BUSINESS

Your business's name is a big deal. It's the first thing a customer encounters when they learn about your business, and it will create their priceless first impression of you. It may also have surprising effects, such as affecting the amount of competition you face to get onto the front page of Internet search results, or determining how far down an alphabetical directory list your business appears. There are also terms and words that are wise to avoid, as many industries are considered high-risk and may result in a lack of funding opportunities.

When selecting your business name, consider questions like:

- Does this name communicate my personality and my brand's personality? If people are drawn to your personality, you want a name that communicates what that personality is.
- Is this name similar to the name of another popular or local brand? That may be a bad thing; your business may face a lot of competition for search engine rankings from that big brand, and customers may even get confused and buy from that other brand instead of from you.
- Could this brand be off-putting to your customers in any way? Some businesses find out too late that a term they used in their name is not viewed as credible or reputable by their audience.

- Is my business a high-risk industry? Avoid using terms like credit repair, trucking, real estate, accounting, cannabis, etc.

Keep these questions in mind as you begin brainstorming potential names for your business.

It's a good idea to start with what BigCommerce.com calls a "word dump." There are probably hundreds of words that could be relevant to your brand and industry. Each word sends a particular message and has a particular personality. Which words are right for your business name?[1]

Try using this checklist to ensure that you get all the juicy words that might apply to your business out on paper.

- Words about what your business does or produces (cookies, computers, lawn care, etc.).
- Words about the experience you want to give your customers (affordable, bliss, easy, power, premium, sweet, etc.)
- Words about any unique aspects of your business model (custom, delivery, rental, name of your town or city if you will serve mostly local customers, etc.).
- Words about the people who run your business (your names, experts, family, geeks, etc.)

Try to come up with a list of at least 100 words to mix, match, brainstorm, and sleep on. In the morning, come up with six to twelve names to ask family, friends, and members of your target customer demographic for their opinions.

Once you have a few favorite names in mind, you will want to check the following:

- Search state records to see if someone is already using this business name in your state. If they are, you probably will not be allowed to register a business with the same name. Each state should have its own name check tool, usually located at an official "state.gov" website. Using your state's official "state.gov" name check tool will help ensure that you are using your state's complete public records, and not a free search offered by a company that may have incomplete information.

- Search federal trademark records to see if someone else has already trademarked the name. These can be searched at: https://tmsearch.uspto.gov
- Check to see if the domain name "yourbusiness.com" is available. If it's not, that may make it harder to drive customers to your website, as they may accidentally end up at the other company's website instead.

Once you have found a name that you love and your target audience seems to like, and you have confirmed that its trademark and domain are available, you're ready to purchase your website domain. I recommend you do this right away, because although it is quicker, cheaper, and easier than registering your business as a legal entity, for all these reasons, a domain name is also more likely to be snatched up by another entrepreneur while you're doing your business registration paperwork!

Of note, most domain names should not cost much more than $20 per year to register. If you find that an unscrupulous business such as a domain "squatter" is demanding hundreds or thousands of dollars in exchange for your domain name, it may be worth contacting the company squatting on the domain to tell them that what they're doing is probably illegal.

"Domain squatting," or the practice of buying a domain and then demanding many times the domain name's market value from anyone who wants to buy it, is indeed illegal in the U.S. in most cases.[2] Some profiteers do it anyway, hoping that people will pay exorbitant prices for the domains they've acquired without realizing that the practice is illegal. If such a company fears a legal challenge, they may release the domain you are interested in back to market prices just to avoid potential legal trouble.

It's also worth noting that your name doesn't *have* to be "yourcompanyname.com." There is no legal requirement whatsoever around what your domain name must be. It's just that it's more likely that customers will try to get to your website simply by typing "yourcompanyname.com" without even checking what your official website domain is, so owning that domain is the best way to ensure that these customers can find you.

Once you've chosen your business's name and made sure you own your business's website domain name, what next?

OBTAINING A BUSINESS ADDRESS

During the process of registering a business, you will likely be asked for a mailing address to which your state will send important legal documents from time to time. In some states, this mailing address may also become a matter of public record in a searchable database. It's a good idea to search your own state's laws and determine if this is true for your state.

If you are concerned about your personal address becoming a matter of public record, here are some ways to obtain a business mailing address without having to make your personal address public or rent a whole office or storefront:

- Virtual office spaces are businesses that may provide mailing addresses, receptionist services, workspaces, and more to small businesses. This allows you to work from anywhere without having to take on the full cost of renting an office or storefront. The mail you receive may be forwarded to your residential address or may be available for pickup at a local location.
- UPS and the U.S. Postal Service are among the entities that offer rental mailboxes. These can include both standard P.O. boxes, and the USPS's "street

addressing" option, which allows you to give out the
address of the post office where your P.O. box is
located as a full mailing address.
- Some coworking spaces may also rent mailboxes out
or offer address services.
- Assign a registered agent.

If you don't have a store or office space to use as a mailing
address and you don't want your residential address to be listed
as part of public record, procuring one of these options for your
business prior to filing your articles of incorporation may be a
good investment.

Once you've got your name, your domain name, and your
mailing address, you have everything you need to officially
create your business as a legal entity. Now, what kind of legal
entity will you choose to incorporate?

CHOOSE A BUSINESS STRUCTURE

There are different business "structures" to which different laws
about tax, liability and other matters apply. These different structures are designed to give different advantages and place
different regulations on businesses of different sizes, with
different numbers of owners and different types of business
activities, etc.

It's a good idea to do further research about which business
structure will be ideal for your business beyond just reading this
book. Until you have a chance to do that, an extremely brief run-
down of the most common types of business structures for new
business owners is as follows:

- Doing Business As. This piece of paper allows you to
do business under a fictional name, such as a pen
name, a performer name, or a business name, without
having to create a separate legal entity for that
business. I do NOT recommend you use a DBA for our

purposes because a DBA will not allow you to obtain the legal standing you need to build business credit. However, it is an option that can be confusing, so I wanted to clarify its purpose.

- Sole Proprietorship. Sole proprietorships are the default type of business you are running if you are running a business by yourself and have not incorporated another type of business entity. Freelancers and other self-employed people who don't work for a corporation are generally legally considered sole proprietors.
- This can make filing taxes easy, but sole proprietorships do nothing to shield the business owner from legal or financial liability. A sole proprietor's personal assets are not protected if their business should go bankrupt or be sued. This is why many sole proprietors eventually create an LLC or other corporation for their business.
- General Partnership. A general partnership is similar to a sole proprietorship in that it is the default business entity that is formed when two or more people start doing business together. In some places, a general partnership is automatically considered to exist if two people are doing business together, even if you haven't filed any paperwork.
- The drawbacks to a general partnership are similar to those of a sole proprietorship. Partners aren't protected from debt or liability, so their personal assets can be seized in the event of bankruptcy or lawsuit. This can be especially dicey because one partner can even be held responsible for business debts incurred by the other partner without their knowledge. This is another reason why LLCs are popular.
- Limited Liability Corporation. This is a common choice for new small businesses. Limited Liability Corporations are the simplest legal entities that offer

some legal protections to their operators and are eligible for Employer Identification Numbers, business bank accounts, business credit, and all the general perks and privileges of a corporation.

- Unlike other corporation types, LLCs generally do not require a board of directors or have strict rules about corporate proceedings.
- S-Corporation. S-Corporations offer certain benefits, such as tax advantages and the ability of the company to sell stock shares to investors. However, S-Corps are subject to stricter rules and regulations than LLCs and can only have up to 100 shareholders.
- C-Corporation. C-Corporations may be of unlimited size and have an unlimited number of shareholders. They are also subject to stricter oversight rules for this very reason. This is the preferred business structure for business owners who wish their company to go public on the stock market one day, but if that is not part of your business structure, it may be easier to avoid the added rules and regulations with an LLC or S-Corp.

Once you have decided which type of legal entity to create for your business, you will need to file paperwork with a state government to incorporate your new business entity.

Typically, this will be your own state. Most states require corporations to be incorporated and pay taxes *at least* in the state in which they operate, so in most cases incorporating in your own state is the safest and simplest thing to do.

You may have heard of some states incorporating in other states. California, for example, imposes an $800 tax on all businesses, regardless of their size or income, so some businesses look for ways to incorporate in other states. Delaware, by contrast, has a dedicated business court which is renowned for its speed and efficiency in deciding legal matters, so many corporations seek to incorporate in Delaware so that they can claim jurisdiction to use this court system if they should ever get into legal trouble or choose to file a lawsuit themselves. Some investors may even *require* that companies they do business with be incorporated in Delaware to ensure a speedy resolution of any business legal issues.

It is technically possible to incorporate in a state other than the one in which you live if you can find someone in that state to be your "registered agent" and receive important legal documents there.

However, realistically speaking, you will have to pay taxes and comply with the laws in both the state in which your business operates and the state in which it incorporates. So, unless you are looking for certain specific legal benefits only granted by some states, it may be safest and easiest to incorporate only in your own state to begin with.[3]

Your state's official "state.gov" website should have a section for business owners seeking to file articles of incorporation in the state. This should provide the paperwork needed to incorporate in your state.

Note that while many online legal services may offer to help you file your articles of incorporation in your state for a fee, it is not necessary to pay a company to help you with this. You can do so if you want the extra assistance, but any individual can fill out articles of incorporation for themselves and submit them directly to their state government.

OBTAINING AN EMPLOYER IDENTIFICATION NUMBER

Employer Identification Numbers are like Social Security Numbers for businesses. As the name implies, one major purpose of these is for use in record keeping related to paying employees and subcontractors. However, just like a Social Security Number, your business will also need one of these to prove its identity when applying for and building credit.

Like Social Security Numbers, Employer Identification Numbers are administered at the federal level. The official federal IRS website, IRS.gov, is the home of information about EINs and how to apply for them.

According to IRS.gov, the person applying for an EIN must have a valid personal Taxpayer Identification Number such as a Social Security Number or an Individual Taxpayer Identification Number. This is designed to ensure that you are real and that the EIN is not being applied for by a fabricated person or an alias.

Having any other information you may need, such as your business's mailing address, is also a good idea.

When you have your Taxpayer Identification Number and business mailing address on hand, you must apply for an EIN by filling out the IRS's online EIN application. The IRS website does not allow you to save your progress on this application, so it's a good idea to set aside some time when you can sit down at your computer and finish this application from start to finish.

Once the application is done, you will want to download, save, and print your EIN application confirmation screen for your records.[4]

You can also apply for an EIN by filling out and snail mailing paper forms to the IRS if you do not have a computer with an Internet connection, but these paper forms can take weeks to be processed by the IRS and can take much longer to correct if any errors have been made in the application. For this reason, I recommend filing online if possible.

Once your articles of incorporation have been approved by your state government and your EIN has been approved by the federal government, congratulations! Your baby business is now a legal entity eligible for its own bank account and business credit lines!

There are just a few more things you will want to have to build your image as a reputable company and ensure proper handling of your business finances.

While it is technically and legally possible to use your personal phone as your business phone number, there are several reasons *not* to do this.

One is the risk of harassment: by using your personal phone number with your customers and clients, you are opening yourself up to receive calls from the public 24 hours a day.

The professional image of your business may also suffer if you answer business phone calls the same way you would answer personal calls, or if you mistake one for the other. Using a landline number instead of a cell phone is important to establish business credibility and national or international presence. It also gives you the ability to use the convenience of an interactive voice response system to direct your callers.

Lastly, if you want a business partner or employee to *also* have access to your business phone line, you don't want this to require that you give them access to use your personal phone unsupervised. It may become burdensome to be the only person who can answer the phone and take down messages for your business, and giving others access to your personal phone and voicemail may be even riskier.

Fortunately, there are a growing number of ways to obtain a business phone number affordably or for free. These include:

- Obtain a toll-free number from a phone provider. This will cost money just like any ordinary phone line would, but it can give you a professional toll-free number, or a custom vanity number that is easy for your customers to remember.
- Companies like kall8.com, Ring Central, Vonage, or your phone provider should offer options, including forwarding your business calls to different phones at different times and creating an automated menu to help direct calls to different people or departments.

If your business does not yet have the need or the budget for a traditional phone line, other options, such as a Google Voice number allow you to set up a free phone number which can be redirected to different physical phones, and free voicemail box which can be checked by different individuals via an online portal.

These free services are more limited in their capabilities than paid phone lines, but they may be useful for businesses which do not receive much phone traffic and which require flexibility in terms of who can make and receive business calls.[5]

Note that not all phone numbers which are registered with a phone company are automatically listed in the national 411 directory. It is important that you are listed in the national directory because this is what lenders will use to verify your business name, address, and phone number. Cell phones are not eligible to be listed in this directory which is another great reason to use a toll-free number. You can register your business with the national 411 directory at listyourself.net and wait about a week for it to be published before checking registration.

It's also important to note that Google Voice numbers are usually not eligible to be listed in 411 information directories. These phone numbers are classified differently from landlines or mobile numbers that are linked to physical phones. This is another reason to get a paid business phone line if possible.

WEBSITE & EMAIL

Remember when we purchased your business domain name? Now it's time to use it. We live in a digital age, and it is likely that most of your customers find and interact with their service providers primarily online. For this reason, it is vital that you have a professional-looking website which contains all the information and features your customers need to make it as easy as possible for them to decide to buy from you. Essential website features include:

- A landing page that gives customers a good idea of what you offer and makes it easy for them to learn more about—and be tempted to buy—your products and services.
- An email address collection feature that allows you to build a mailing list of people you can contact with special offers and news about new products and services. You may wish to offer a coupon or a useful free download, known as a "lead magnet," as an incentive for customers to give you their email addresses.
- A page of Frequently Asked Questions that answers the ten or so most common questions or objections that may stop customers from buying from you. Try to address whatever the most common concerns for customers in your industry might be.
- If possible, an online store allowing customers to order products or book services from you right on your website. If a customer can make an impulse buy online, they are more likely to come back to you again and again.
- There are many services available to help you do this, including services that arrange online retail shipping, services that allow customers to book appointments with you using an automated calendar, and services that coordinate local food delivery.
- Your hours of operation should be listed so that customers know when they can expect your business to be open.
- Your business phone number should be listed so that customers can call you with questions.
- If possible, an online live chat feature where customers can ask questions quickly just by typing a message. Some web hosts offer messaging services which will direct these messages to an app on your phone so that you or your associates can text back promptly without

having to pay a full-time customer support agent.
Chatbots are a great option too.

- At some point you will probably want to invest in
  Search Engine Optimization to help you show up
  higher in search engine results. However, this doesn't
  need to be done right away if search engine results are
  not expected to be your major source of customers and
  sales.
- While you are making your website, it is a good idea
  to also make a Google Maps profile for your business.
  This profile will allow customers to find your business
  if they are searching for products or services in your
  industry near your geographic location. It will also
  allow customers to leave and read reviews, and give
  you a place to encourage people to post good reviews
  of your business.

These are just a few features that are helpful to have on your business website. None of them are legally required, but all of them will help you to build and engage your audience and make more sales.

There are many web hosts out there which offer different benefits for different types of businesses. However, to be honest, I recommend Squarespace, because it is affordable and makes it fairly easy to incorporate all of these features into a beautiful-looking website.

I'm not affiliated with Squarespace or anything—I've just found them to be the best mix of value and affordability for business owners who are new to web design. If you already know a lot about web design, you may have other preferences based on hosts which will allow you more affordability or more flexibility that you can make use of with your expertise.

OBTAINING A BUSINESS E-MAIL ADDRESS

Many website hosting packages will offer one or more email addresses with "@yourbusiness.com" as their domain. This can be a very good option since it gives your business the air of official credibility that comes with having websites hosted at your domain name.

You can create email addresses such as "info@yourbusiness.com," or "yourname@yourbusiness.com," depending on what will best suit your customer's needs and the image you want to project.

If you don't want to pay for "@yourdomain.com" email addresses, you can also make free email addresses using other services, such as Gmail or Google Workspace, to serve as the email address for your business. This looks slightly less professional since everyone knows that these addresses are free and anyone can make them, but there is nothing technically or legally wrong with using such free addresses and they may serve your customers just fine.

But whatever you do, don't go without a business website and email address. These are likely to be the most common way customers want to find and communicate with you, so you want to ensure you have these channels in place as soon as possible!

OBTAINING BUSINESS LICENSES AND PERMITS

I will be honest here: business licenses can be quite confusing. This is because different states and even different cities may have different requirements for what kinds of businesses need what kinds of licenses. The simplest way to determine what the requirements for your specific business are probably to search "what licenses do you need to operate a _______ business in <insert your city and state here>."

Almost all cities and states will require businesses with potential health or financial implications for customers and employees, such as food-related businesses, businesses involving the use of heavy machinery, cosmetic or wellness services, and certain types of accountants or financial advisors, to have some kind of license.

Some cities may require licenses for just about any type of business, such as San Francisco's requirement that all electronics repair businesses have a special license since there are possible safety hazards from incorrectly repaired electronics. Some businesses, like car washing and car repair, may require a business license in some cities but not others.

If your business has a physical location or uses certain types of supplies or machinery, there is a good chance you will also need a permit. Different kinds of businesses may need to meet different kinds of requirements for fire safety, safe disposal of potentially hazardous waste, safe handling of potentially hazardous chemicals, and more. Again, these requirements will vary by state.

It is especially important to make sure that you know the safety requirements for spaces in your industry *before* renting or buying an office or retail space. Business owners can end up in a tight spot if they buy or rent a retail space and then discover, for example, that it does not meet the local fire safety regulations for the type of products they plan to sell. These regulations can vary by industry, so a food service business may need a space with different fire safety ratings from a retail business.

The only way to know what kinds of licenses and permits your business will need is to research your city and state's specific requirements. Be sure that you know this information before you start selling goods or services, as the fines and penalties for operating a business that requires a license without one can be hefty.

This system may seem burdensome at times but try to have patience with it. Remember: all these licenses and permits are ultimately for the safety of customers, employees, and residents. You wouldn't want a business operating using toxic chemicals or fire hazards near your home without a license proving that they had met safety requirements, and you wouldn't want to do business with a professional "expert" only to find that they weren't actually able to pass licensure tests for their industry. So please ensure you meet all the requirements yourself as a responsible business owner.

BUSINESS BANK ACCOUNT

In order to obtain business credit and funding, your business will need to have its own bank account. Fortunately, this is easy to procure once your articles of incorporation and your EIN application have been approved by your state and federal governments. You will also likely need documentation of any business licenses that your city and state require for businesses in your industry, so that your potential business credit lines can verify that your business is legitimate and properly licensed.

Once everything is properly registered with the appropriate government agencies, your business will be eligible for the same kinds of financial accounts as you are, and then some. Types of accounts your business may need include:

- A checking account. This is an account from which your business can directly withdraw money to pay expenses.
- A savings account. This is an account where your business can save money for long-term goals that is not available for daily spending purposes.
- A credit card account. This is a line of business credit to which expenses can be charged.
- A merchant services account. This is a type of account used by businesses to *accept* payments from customers. Deposits can be made to this account through your payment methods.

Before opening your bank accounts, you will want to check the offers available to businesses through local banks. Although it may seem simpler to set up your business bank accounts through the same bank as your personal accounts, that may not always get you the best offer and all the features that would benefit your business.

When deciding what bank to use, compare features like:

- Any monthly fees these banks may levy on business bank accounts.
- Minimum balances that may need to be maintained to avoid bank fees.
- Interest rates you earn on money in your accounts.
- Interest rates you pay on money owed on your business credit card.
- Any transaction fees or termination fees to end your credit line.
- Introductory offers such as offers of signup bonuses or low interest rates.
- Rewards programs such as business credit cards that grant you points to buy things that are useful for your industry. Some banks may offer credit cards that offer specific types of rewards tailored to businesses in specific industries.

Once you have selected the bank that you believe offers your business the best deal, you will need to present the following documentation to open an account in the name of your business entity:

- Your business's EIN or other Tax Identification Number.
- Proof of incorporation if your business is, indeed, a corporation.
- Any business licenses or registrations required by your city or state.
- Proof of address for the address at which you plan to receive bank correspondence about your business.

- Proof of identification as the owner of your business, such as a driver's license, passport, or state identification card.

When you have your documentation gathered, it's time to go to the bank to open your accounts.

At this time your business will not have any credit history, but don't worry. We will add new business credit lines as we go and investigate potential upgrades to your existing business credit line throughout this book. Since your business is now an official legal entity, we can do it all without risking or harming your personal credit.

If you already have pretty good personal credit, minimal hard inquiries, and are confident in approval, this may be an opportune time to apply for a business credit card as a personal guarantor. This means that you may be asked to personally guarantee that you will repay money borrowed by your business.

This is a kind of business credit to be especially careful with. Don't take out loans or rack up charges you can't afford to pay back at this time, since this may affect your personal credit as the guarantor. But using this line of credit reliably to make and pay back small business purchases will allow you to start building business credit history immediately.

I probably don't need to tell you to use your business credit line and all your business accounts responsibly. Don't make personal deposits or purchases using your business accounts. This will ensure that you do not get taxed twice or fined by the IRS. Your personal and business finances should always be kept entirely separate.

If you plan to spend money your business makes for personal reasons, do it by paying yourself a "salary" from the business account rather than by charging personal purchases directly to your business bank accounts. Charging personal purchases to a business account could raise suspicions of embezzlement or fraud, and you don't want that!

Now that you have a business bank account, you are eligible

for other types of business credit lines that we will discuss throughout this book. These accounts will ask you to apply for credit using your EIN and may ask you to pay off your business credit lines using your business bank account.

Having a business bank account is the safest and easiest way to grow your business' credit score, since it is a wall of separation between your business and personal finances. This allows you to grow your business' credit score independent of your personal credit score and keep your business's money separate.

This independence protects your personal credit score and assets in case of bankruptcy, and allows co-owners and future owners of your business access to the benefits of your business's credit since these things are no longer dependent on your personal finances.

There is one last thing you will probably need to start and run a successful business. I cannot give you a comprehensive course on this subject in the space of just one book, but I want you to be set up to succeed so I am going to address it briefly.

Know that there are many courses on this final subject available to you online, and local organizations such as your local SCORE administration office may even be able to offer you free expert help with this last vital component.

This last vital component is your business plan.

WRITING A BUSINESS PLAN

In its simplest form, a business plan is a document where you write down exactly how you plan to make a profit from your business. This document will most often be requested by banks when seeking a business loan or certain other types of credit lines. It will also be requested by investors if you choose to seek those in the future. Its function is to help you create a realistic plan to optimize the growth of your business, and to prove to others that your business is worth investing in.

Nine common components of a business plan include:

1. An executive summary. Think of this as an "elevator pitch" telling people what's great about your business. Include your company's mission statement, a summary of the products and services it offers, and a broad summary of your financial growth plans. You may wish to draft an executive summary first, then revisit and rewrite it after you have finished the other components to update it with any discoveries you have made along the way.

2. A company description. This more detailed technical description should include components like your business's full registered name, its mailing address and phone number, and the names of key people on your team.

3. Be sure to highlight the expertise brought by each team member so you can show potential lenders and investors your business' unique expertise, and you can keep your team's strengths in mind throughout the rest of the business planning process. If different people own different percentages or shares of your company, include information about who owns what as well.

4. A section on business goals. These should include some specific short-term goals so that all lenders or investors will understand what their investments in your business will be used for.

5. These should not be financial goals such as "make X amount of money," but rather goals that will help you *bring in* cash flow, such as launching a new product or service line, opening a new location, or launching a new marketing strategy to drastically expand your customer base. Include specific numbers such as the number of new customers you hope to recruit or the anticipated revenue from your new product line or location.

6. Detailed description of products and services. Here you will want to get into the details and the math of how your company will turn a profit. Include the following details:

7. An explanation of how your product or service is delivered to the customer.

8. The pricing model for your products and services, including the cost to provide these and the profit margin when customers buy them.

9. A description of the customers you serve and advertise to.

10. Your supply chain and order fulfillment strategy.

11. Your sales and marketing strategies, and the costs and return on investment so far if these strategies are already active.

12. Your distribution strategy.

13. Any patents or trademarks your company may own or have in process.

14. Do your market research. Lenders and investors will want to know what sets your company apart from the competition, and who your company appeals to. You will want to research and discuss factors including:

15. Who is your target audience, and why will they buy from you rather than other suppliers?

16. Who is your competition, what do they do well, and what do you do better than them?

17. Any important details about your target audience, such as whether they are an underserved market or whether you have identified an unmet need.

18. Outline your marketing and sales plan. This will include any methods you may use to bring in new customers, including deploying sales professionals, visual attractions in your storefront window, coupons and special offers for first-time customers, using online or other paid ads that reach target audiences in their everyday lives.

19. Include components that convert new customers into
    loyal customers such as loyalty programs, a sequence
    of discounts or special offers to incentivize repeat
    sales, personalized offers and interactions to cultivate
    personal relationships with the customers, etc..
20. If you have already put some of these into practice,
    report on their return on investment so far. This is easy
    to track if you are using online ads with click-tracking
    and purchase-tracking, but may be harder to track and
    optimize for methods such as billboards or radio ads.
21. Perform a business financial analysis. If you are
    already making sales and already have data on profit-
    and-loss and return on investment, include this
    information here. If you have them, you will want to
    include metrics like:
22. Net profit margin.
23. Current ratio of your liquidity and your ability to pay
    debts.
24. Accounts receivable turnover ratio.

Using graphs and infographics may help to drive home any
positive points about your business' finances.

If you don't know what some of the above terms mean right
now, that's okay. But you will want to research them. They are
useful tools for predicting and optimizing a business's profits,
and the more of these tools you master, the more profit you are
likely to be able to bring in.

1. Make financial projections. In a big way, this is the
   final and most important act of your business plan.
   Everything else has been building up to this.
2. Your lenders and investors will want to know with as
   much certainty as possible that you will be able to pay
   them back and provide a return on their investment.
   So here is where you must show that your business
   will make a profit.

3. I advise that you *not* be overly optimistic on this
   section. It may be tempting to do so if you are trying to
   entice investors or lenders, but this business plan is
   also for *you*. You will do better if you underestimate
   your earnings and subsequently find ways to cut costs
   and improve your profit margin than if you
   overestimate your sales and profit margin and spend
   more money than you make.
4. So be conservative here. If you want to make your
   financial projections as impressive as possible, do that
   by finding ways to *increase* your profit margins
   through optimization and innovation. Not by
   artificially pumping them up with dubious hopes and
   assumptions.
5. If you already have quarterly reports, use these to
   illustrate how much your business is making and
   how much you expect it to grow when new
   products, locations, or marketing strategies are
   added.

If you do not already have quarterly reports, project as accurately as you can what you expect your business revenue to look like based on a realistic projection of your costs, profit margins, and the number of customers served over time.

It is not unusual for new businesses to take losses in their first two years, so if you cannot show profit right away, that is not the end of the world. But you will want to convincingly show that you can create a substantial and growing profit margin within two years—for your sake and that of the banks and investors.

You can download sample business plans to help you see exactly what to do for free from the website of the U.S. Small Business Administration at:

https://www.sba.gov/business-guide/plan-your-business/write-your-business-plan

Whew! That chapter was a doozy. But after completing it,

you should have everything you need to establish a fully functioning business and begin building your business credit score.

Now it's time to talk about the bedrock of business credit: your business credit report. Just like with your personal credit, your business credit report is where all the information about your available credit and payment history will appear. It is the report that your potential lenders, vendors, and investors will consult when deciding whether doing business with you is a profitable proposition.

CHAPTER 3
ESTABLISH (AND FIX!) YOUR BUSINESS CREDIT REPORTS

It's an intimidating fact that banks turn away about 80% of all businesses that come to them looking for a business loan.[1] When this happens, it's usually because the bank is afraid the business owner will not be able to make a profit and pay them back. Even if you don't need or plan to take out a business loan, this reflects the harsh reality that financial professionals don't always expect businesses to succeed and grow.

The good news is the same measures that will give your business a great credit score can also help your business to grow in all aspects by ensuring a proper focus on profit and financial growth.

If you are seeking a business loan, following the best practices for building your credit score can help put you in the top 20% of most prepared loan applicants. The same steps also place your business among the most likely to succeed, not just because of the availability of loans, but because following these best practices will get you to rigorously manage your business's finances and profit margin.

You may know that in your personal life, your credit report is like a report card for your history of paying your bills. Having multiple open lines of credit with a stellar history of on-time payments will build up your credit score quickly, while any bill you don't pay may be reported to credit bureaus and harm your credit score.

Credit scores can be frustrating because the system used to determine them is arbitrary and even a little bit secretive. For example, no one knows exactly what formula the Fair Isaacs Company (FICO) uses to calculate business credit scores. However, we have a fairly reliable understanding of what actions will help or harm your business credit report.

This chapter is about building an excellent credit report so your business can obtain the best deals, interest rates, and loans to help you grow.

The importance of a good credit score to a business cannot be overstated. Just like your personal credit, your business credit can determine things like:

- Whether your business can be approved for business loans, and how long the approval process will take.
- What interest rates you receive on business loans—in other words, how much money you end up paying the lender for the privilege of taking out a loan.
- How much money you are authorized to borrow to grow your business.
- Which landlords are willing to rent office space and other properties to your business.
- Whether investors are willing to invest money in your business.
- Whether major vendors are willing to do business with you.

So who calculates business credit scores, and how are they different from personal credit scores?

THE FICO SMALL BUSINESS SCORING SERVICE

The FICO Small Business Scoring Service, or FICO SBSS, awards businesses credit scores of between 0-300. These scores are used to make important decisions: for example, as of this writing the U.S. Small Business Administration will only consider making loans to businesses with a FICO SBSS of 140 or above. Businesses with a credit score of 160 or above have the best chance of being approved for an SBA-backed loan.

For a new business owner, your personal credit score can serve as the foundation for your business credit score. Since a new business has no credit history of its own, its owner's personal credit score may be used to determine what lines of credit the business is eligible for. However, be aware that too many hard inquiries often hurt business owners in the long run and take a long time to either remove or fall off.

The statutory limit for hard inquiries to remain on a personal credit report is two years. Applying for your first lines of business credit with a personal credit score of less than 600 may not be the best decision. Business owners with lower personal credit scores may be subjected to higher interest rates and other unfavorable terms when applying for business credit—meaning you'll pay more back for each dollar of business credit you obtain. This can slow the growth of a business and can make financial problems in the future more likely.

Having a personal credit score of over 700 is ideal when applying for personally guaranteed funds. Business owners with scores in this range will most likely get the best credit and financing deals. This can have a major impact on how much startup capital you can raise, what your profit margin on that capital is, and more.

Note that I say "ideal" here because, again, personal credit score is not always *necessary* to this process. If you want to start building revolving business credit or obtain loans right away, you can apply for lines of business credit that require a personal credit score, especially if you are already cash-flowing.

That's why I advise that people looking to start building their business get their personal credit into good shape first or during the business credit-building process. If you struggle with your personal credit score, or just aren't sure about it, my first book,

The Credit Game: Plays We Were Never Taught, covers how personal credit scores are determined as well as some of the easiest ways to build your personal credit scores up fast.

This may be an especially good idea since having good personal and business credit may help you get the best options in the higher tiers of business credit which you will become eligible for four to six months from now if you follow the steps in this book. Working on your personal credit alongside your business credit will put you in the best possible position when this time comes.

Just be sure you keep straight which of your credit-building accounts are for your business and which are personal so there isn't any confusion at tax time!

Once you've taken the steps from Chapter 2 to obtain a stable business foundation, you are ready to start building up a business credit score that will make you eligible for bigger and better loans and credit lines, as well as protect your personal finances and help your business appeal to investors.

When determining your SBSS, FICO will look at factors including:

- The personal credit history of the business's owners.
- The business's own credit history if it already has a credit history.
- Business financial data such as the business's assets and liabilities, cash flow, revenue, etc.
- The amount of time a business has existed. Most new businesses fail in their first three years, so simply showing that you've been in business longer than that may be considered evidence that you know how to manage your business's finances. If your business is brand new, though, don't worry—the other measures we take will more than compensate for this.
- Any negative marks against the business's payment history, such as past liens or judgments rendered against your business for non-payment of bills.

It's worth noting here that FICO uses different processes for evaluating small, medium-sized, and big businesses. This is important because otherwise, larger businesses would have a huge advantage over small businesses due to their larger cash flows and larger assets.

Since FICO considers business size when making credit score determinations, a sole proprietor freelancer can have the same FICO score as Walmart if they play their cards right, and can be just as likely to get approved for a loan![2]

HOW DO YOU BUILD YOUR FICO SBSS?

Remember how we said that a business credit score of 140 was necessary to be considered for an SBA-backed business loan? Good news! A business owner with a stellar personal credit score and excellent business cash flow can obtain a business credit score of 140 even if they just started their business last month and have no prior business credit history.

This is encouraging for any small business owner who is intimidated by the thought of entering the business credit game. However, 140 is the very minimum business credit score that may qualify you for SBA-backed loans. To have higher chances of getting more loans with better interest rates and higher credit limits, you will want to build your business credit in much the same way you would build your personal credit. For new businesses, there are two major ways to do this:

1. Maintain your personal credit. Sole proprietorships and new businesses are especially vulnerable to taking credit score hits if their owner's personal credit score drops.
2. Signing up for new lines of credit such as net 30 accounts, revolving credit accounts, and more. Throughout the rest of this book, we will cover which account types to apply to over the upcoming months to maximize your business credit score.

3. Just be sure not to mix in any personal transactions. Using business credit cards for personal expenses is a huge red flag for the IRS and credit bureaus and may cause your business to be seen as too risky to lend to or invest in.

Just like with your personal credit, there are more ways to build business credit. Any loans your business eventually takes out will determine how reliable your business is as a lender.

Businesses with prior histories of successfully paying back loans are more likely to be granted bigger financing with better interest rates in the future. However, I recommend that business owners who are new to business credit use business credit cards to build up their business credit scores and optimize their business spending habits before applying for loans or other types of financing.

Net 30 accounts are a low-risk way of borrowing money and showing you can pay it back because you are in control of exactly how much you charge on your business credit card each month. You can charge just a small amount each month on multiple net 30 accounts, showing that you can handle multiple payments responsibly and so can be trusted with future larger credit lines and financing.

On the other hand, loans and cash credit often involve agreeing to pay a significant amount back to the lender monthly on a long-term basis. This can be a struggle for new businesses that are just establishing their customer base or aren't used to handling bills from lenders. So not only will a new business with less credit history likely be asked to pay higher interest rates on a business loan—newer businesses may struggle to pay off their loans or high-limit credit lines on time which can harm their business credit history.

Try working your way up to a business credit score of 160 or higher through the maintenance of excellent personal credit and the strategic use of business credit cards before you apply for a loan or another type of high-risk financing. The more practice you have paying off creditors and the higher your business credit score when you apply, the more likely you will qualify for loans with great interest rates that you can use to grow.

The FICO SBSS is one of the most widely used business credit scores, so it's a good one to start paying attention to first. However, other organizations also offer business credit reporting and these may also be useful for business owners to be aware of.

HOW TO FIX BUSINESS CREDIT

If your business already has some negative marks on its credit history, you can begin repairing those and establishing a positive credit history today. Some strategies for doing so are obvious, such as paying all your bills on time and in full to establish an excellent payment history. Other strategies, however, might not be so obvious. I want to share a few tips here.

Steps you can take today to improve your business credit score include:

1. Making payments in full and on time. This is the easiest way to avoid accumulating negative marks in the first place.
2. Reduce your debt on revolving credit accounts. "Revolving credit" refers to accounts where your charges and balance can change monthly. This typically means credit cards or other lines of credit where you can charge various amounts and pay various amounts each month.
3. Owing a lot in credit card debt or other revolving lines of credit can lower your business credit score. So, one quick way to raise it is to begin paying those debts off as quickly as possible, even if you are not technically required to do so according to the terms of the credit line. Remember, our goal here is to please the credit reporting agencies—not just the credit card company.

4. In general, credit reporting agencies will give higher scores to businesses that owe less than 20% or 30% of their credit limit on each line of credit they possess. For the fastest results, take some time to review your credit lines and determine the fastest way to pay off your debts so you owe less than 30% of your limit on each business credit line you have.

5. Once you have gotten each business credit line you have down below 30% utilization, work on getting them all as close to zero as possible. It's not bad to owe a little money, but the less existing business credit debt you have, the more flexibility you will have to pay future unexpected costs or growth costs. Your card companies will also be more likely to raise your credit limit after paying in full each month.

6. Rehabilitate past-due accounts. Did you know that you can often negotiate with creditors or submit disputes directly through the bureaus (recommended) to have negative marks removed from your business credit report? Creditors will not normally advertise the fact that they offer this, but if you ask, they are often willing to negotiate in exchange for payment. However, disputing with the bureaus is often a lot quicker and easier than dealing with creditors.

7. Creditors want to get paid first and foremost. For that reason, they might agree to update their reporting to credit scoring agencies to remove negative marks if you make a certain number of payments in full and on time moving forward. This arrangement, sometimes called "pay for delete," which is just that. You pay the creditor in exchange for the deletion of negative marks from your credit score.

8. Open new credit accounts. Having a larger number of credit lines can improve your credit score by showing that you have existing sources of money to borrow from to pay off any new lenders.

9. Don't just spam business credit providers with applications—applying for a new line of credit usually results in your score losing a few points, so applying too many lines of credit in a short span of time is a bad idea. But by strategically applying for credit lines that you are likely to qualify for, you can increase your number of open accounts over time. The more credit accounts you pay off on time each month, the faster your credit score will rise.

10. That's why I recommend that when you obtain a new line of credit, you charge a small amount to that credit line and pay it on time each month. This is easiest if you set the credit card to autopay so that it will automatically be paid off in full each month without you having to manually remember to pay your bill.

11. Add positive trade references to your Dun and Bradstreet account. Not all vendors, suppliers, or business partners automatically report their information to credit reporting agencies. Some creditors often only report to bureaus when there's a problem, and that means these agencies might not know about all the on-time payments you've made.

12. Fortunately, Dun and Bradstreet allows you to report your own accounts, such as accounts with suppliers, vendors, and business partners, for inclusion on their report. In this way you can get credit for the on-time payments you're already making and improve your Dun and Bradstreet Paydex score.

13. Keep personal and business finances separate. It can sometimes be hard to adjust to using different payment methods for personal vs. business expenses, especially if you are used to paying your business expenses out of your own pocket. But it's essential that you keep these finances separate for several reasons.

14. Mixing personal and business finances is a huge red fl ag for the IRS. Using business funds for personal

expenses and confusing personal expenses for business deductions can be considered fraud, or even embezzlement. Though there's a clear moral difference between intentionally embezzling large amounts of funds and accidentally using the wrong credit card for personal expenses, the legal ramifications can be the same.

15. Mixing business and personal finances can also put both credit scores at risk. Your business credit score may suffer due to personal expenses being posted to your business account, which can make it harder to secure business deals and funding in the future.

16. You can seek a secured bank loan if all else fails. If your company badly needs funds or new credit lines to raise its credit score and it doesn't qualify for an unsecured loan, you may still be able to obtain a secured loan to keep the lights on and build up a successful payment history.

17. A "secured" loan is a loan where the lender knows they will recoup what they have paid you because you have promised to forfeit assets to them if you are unable to pay them back any other way. You may be able to offer assets such as a car or property you own as collateral, forfeiting ownership of these assets to the lender in the event you can't pay the loan back.

18. Obviously, this is something to be careful with as it can put your personal assets at risk. But it can also serve as a last line of leverage if you need to get a loan on record in order to build up your payment history and you can't get an unsecured line of credit. But before agreeing to it, make sure you can pay off this secured loan without going further into debt that may harm your credit history.

19. Business tradelines are another great option that are similar to being added to someone else's personal credit card account as an authorized user only for the

business. Depending on the source, these accounts can give a good boost and be temporary to permanent.

As you can see here, there are several ways you can add positive credit history to your business credit reports, and there are even ways to remove reports of late payments you've made in the past. But, what can you do if negative marks on your business's credit report don't even rightfully belong to your business?

ADDRESSING MISTAKES ON BUSINESS CREDIT REPORTS

Unfortunately, as with personal credit reports, errors and identity theft can also happen with business credit reports. The chances of this can increase if you accidentally provide incorrect information to a bureau, such as an incorrectly spelled name or an incorrect Employer Identification Number. They can also increase if other individuals or businesses have the same name as yours, leading to potential confusion of identity.

These incorrect items can have severe impacts on your business's prospects. Incorrect reports of unpaid bills, legal actions against your business, or other negative items can make it harder to find lenders, investors, vendors, and office space. How can you fix these problems on your business credit report if you have no control over the unpaid bills or negative actions that are being incorrectly reported as yours?

Every credit report provider is legally required to have a process to allow you to dispute incorrect items on your report. The dispute process is designed to remove incorrect items so that business credit reports are accurate.

In theory, this dispute process is generally simple and involves contacting the scoring agency which put the inaccurate item on your credit report. In practice, however, in some cases it can be quite complicated and difficult to get the mistake corrected. Credit scoring agencies may be reluctant to admit to mistakes or to expend the time and effort to comb through records to verify your claims.

Just as in personal credit, there is a science to disputing errors on your business credit reports. This science involves knowing the law around what credit reporting agencies are legally required to do for you, and demonstrating to them that you know the law. The dispute process may require contacting the agency multiple times over the course of months and using specific legal language to demonstrate that you know the law and will legally pursue the matter if the agency doesn't take appropriate action.

This is one area where my business, Major League Credit & Lending, can offer advice and assistance. A big part of our job is knowing the laws around credit reporting and using that knowledge to help clients to remove erroneous items from their business credit reports. Paperwork is also key to proving your case, so always keep an organized paper trail in the event that you may need to pursue legal action.

I will share some tips for managing this process throughout this book, but successfully disputing credit reporting errors can get sufficiently complicated that I could not fit all of the possibilities and recommended courses of action into this book. If you encounter a credit reporting error and do not have success in your initial attempts to get it corrected, don't hesitate to reach out to me to see how I can help.

CHAPTER 4

BUSINESS CREDIT TIER 1: NET 30 ACCOUNTS

Now that you've set your business up as an independent entity with its own credit score and credit reports, it's time to secure your first business credit. I recommend doing this by establishing your first store account with a vendor or supplier.

Store accounts are low-risk for borrowers and lenders alike precisely because they are restricted to buying from only one store.

For you, this means that you are unlikely to spend huge amounts of money and find yourself struggling to pay it back. If you can only use this line of credit on certain items necessary to your business's operation, the risk of budgeting errors or spending money on items that do not have a direct benefit for your business is low.

This, in turn, means that the creditor is less likely to lose money from nonpayment. The creditor is also likely to make more profit by selling you more products over time if they know that you have a special arrangement to buy supplies your business needs from their brand. They win customer loyalty and you win store credit. Everybody wins.

As we mentioned earlier, these come in different varieties, including net 10, net 15, net 30, and net 60. The number in these designations refers to the number of days you have to pay for the purchases you make using these lines of credit. I recommend starting with net 30 accounts to grow your business credit with the best mix of speed and reliability to ensure that your scores are reported to credit bureaus every month while minimizing the chances that you will forget to pay on a payment time.

These lines of credit may seem unimpressive at first glance. Obtaining a line of credit to buy shipping supplies, coffee cups, or car parts may feel less glamorous than obtaining a five- or six-figure bank loan. But that's exactly the point: these lines of credit are easy for anyone with a legal business entity to apply for, and they serve as the proving ground for later more challenging approvals.

Loans also, of course, help you to build your business. When you're first learning your business model and discovering what will be most profitable for you, you don't necessarily want to be making big money moves at that point. You are more likely to get the best possible return on your investment if you do your major spending *after* you have determined how to optimize your profit through trial and error in the early months or years of your business.

For their part, banks and other potential creditors are likely to reject someone with a brand-new business and no credit history who asks for tens of thousands of dollars, but they'll sit up and pay attention if a business owner who already has a history of paying off thousands of dollars per month in trade credit for six months or more offers to pay them *back* tens of thousands of dollars with interest.

When you have an excellent business credit score, banks will have high confidence that you will pay them back, and they may even compete with each other by offering you lower interest rates than the competition.

How do you even find vendors or suppliers offering store credit?

Before you apply for trade/vendor credit, there are a few things you want to know to ensure that you get the desired result.

One thing to know is that it is very, very important that you register for these trade accounts using your business' registered name, EIN, and contact information. This is because the information you use to register your trade accounts will be the information that is also used to verify your business and report to the credit bureaus. For this reason, if you register under a personal name or if there is an error in the business information you submit, your activity on these accounts may not show up on your business's credit report. Any inconsistencies in your business information can also cause you to be denied financing, so make sure everything matches up across the board.

It's also useful to know that only $50 or more charges are reported to credit bureaus in most cases. That means you will want to spend at least that much on each of your tradelines to initially activate them and use them every few months if you want to build a strong, consistent reporting history.

You will also want to look for lenders with favorable terms. So what does a favorable line of trade credit look like?

ATTRIBUTES OF A GOOD LENDER

When opening a tradeline, you should be given information about its net/credit terms. This refers to the term you have to pay your tradeline lender. If you see the term "net 30," for example, that means that you have thirty days to make the agreed-upon payment to your tradeline lender. "Net 60" can mean you have 60 days, and "net 90" means you have 90 days.

Some businesses prefer longer net terms to give them more time to pay off their balances, but it's important to keep in mind that payments are only reported to the credit bureaus as often as they're made. This means that an account with Net 30 terms will report your successful payments to the credit bureaus faster and more frequently than an account with net 90 terms, which may not report your successful payment to the credit bureaus until 90 days after your first purchase with them. Some companies may even offer your business a discount on supplies if you pay your invoice early, so keep an eye out for rewards that could help your dollar go further as a small business!

Knowing when the 30 days you have to pay your invoice begins is also a good idea. When is the start date of this period? Is it the day you make the purchase? The day you receive a digital copy of the invoice? The day an invoice sent via snail mail is postmarked? If you plan to pay your balances early, you may not need to worry about this too much, but it's good information to have and to put into your business calendar to prevent any possibility of accidentally paying late.[1]

For this chapter, we will focus on vendors with two attributes ideal for businesses seeking to build Tier 1 credit history rapidly. These three important attributes are:

1. Net 30 accounts. While some businesses prefer longer or shorter payment periods, net 30 accounts are a fast yet reliable way to build credit history as they report your successful payments to credit bureaus just 30 days after they issue your invoice.
2. Report your payments to at least two of the three major business credit reporting agencies. All the vendors we will recommend here report your successful payments to at least two of the following: Dun & Bradstreet, Equifax, and Experian.

Some examples of businesses that offer reputable tradelines with favorable terms include Wayfair,[2] Quill, and Office Depot.

Quill, for example, specializes in helping new businesses build credit quickly with net 30 terms on a huge variety of items ranging from office supplies to laundry detergent to snacks and hot drinks for the break room.[3]

Office Depot offers a number of credit options for businesses, including a variety of rewards and payment terms which readers can view by following the link in this footnote.[4]

Uline offers tradelines that can be used to purchase supplies, including shipping supplies, packaging materials for retail products, and safety and janitorial supplies.[5]

Grainger is another favored tradeline partner for small business owners, offering tradelines that can be used to purchase tools and supplies for a variety of hardware-intensive industries, including HVAC, plumbing, lawn care and landscaping, laboratory equipment, metalworking, and vehicle maintenance.[6]

You can find many more vendors offering net 30 business credit lines for businesses with little credit history, but these are a few of my favorites.

There are also other resources to help you rapidly build business credit. Here are some other potential good additions to your early business credit portfolio.

ECREDABLE

eCredable is a company that will allow you to report almost any business account to Dun & Bradstreet, Equifax, CreditSafe, Ansonia, and Experian business reports as positive payment history. This can help you rapidly grow your business credit history without requiring you to make new purchases or spend more money.

With a $50 initial setup fee and about $10 per month fee thereafter, eCredable does cost some money but is arguably a good value for the ability to report thousands of dollars in pre-existing bills to these major credit bureaus as credit history each month. You can explore eCredable's options and sign up if you wish using the link in this footnote.[7]

To me, eCredable is an obvious choice for businesses since it allows you to get business credit payment history for potentially thousands of dollars per month in bills you are already paying to landlords, utility companies, and more without needing a high-limit credit card you can charge these items to.

CREDITSTRONG

CreditStrong's business options allow new businesses to take out an interest-free loan for the sole purpose of repaying said loan on time to build credit payment history, which is then reported to credit bureaus. Businesses can borrow $2,500, $5,000, $10,000, or $25,00 and pay anywhere from $100 or $1,100 per month to build loan repayment history without having to qualify for a conventional bank loan.

While CreditStrong's loans are interest-free, they do charge a one-time "administration fee" to set up. This is how they protect their investment : since they are open to new businesses with little credit history, they must assume that some percentage of their borrowers will not successfully repay their loans, so they must protect their cash flow somehow.

For this reason, CreditStrong may not be right for businesses with very tight budgets or those concerned about their ability to repay a loan. But for businesses seeking to build credit history quickly and who have high confidence in their ability to repay the loan amounts in addition to their existing bills, CreditStrong can be a good option to qualify for a loan payment history without needing the credit history to qualify for a conventional loan. Interested parties can view their plan options using the link in the footnotes.[8]

NAV BUSINESS CREDIT SCORES & REPORTS

NAV is a little bit like CreditKarma for businesses. It offers credit monitoring and recommendations for business credit cards, equipment financing, merchant cash advances, and loans your business may qualify for.

I want to note that one should exercise caution when using both Credit Karma and NAV: both sites may be rewarded by creditors for referring borrowers, so not every recommendation they make will be in your best strategic interest. NAV may include lenders encouraging you to borrow more money than you can pay back, or offering you unfavorable terms such as high-interest rates. That's why it's important to read all terms and conditions, carefully plan based on your current cash flow, and be educated about good and bad terms on business credit lines.

That said, if you know the time has come to add a particular type of credit line to your business credit portfolio, NAV can help you find and compare options you qualify for. NAV also offers services, including helping small businesses apply for grants that don't need to be paid back, helping procure business insurance, and assisting with payroll and accounting.

If you have any questions about this process, my team of advisors at Major League Credit & Lending is here to help with a complete business credit-building system.

CHAPTER 5
MONITOR BUSINESS CREDIT REPORTS

Now that you have established your business's credit reports and obtained your first lines of business credit, it's time to think about monitoring your business credit. By monitoring your business credit reports, you can see what lenders see when deciding whether to lend to you—and ensure that what they see looks good.

STEPS TO CREATE A STELLAR CREDIT RATING

Your credit history is the most important component of creating a stellar business credit report. If you do perform all the following steps, there is a good chance that your business credit score will grow and thrive. To build amazing business credit, you will want to:

1. Open more than one line of basic trade credit. This allows you to be documented by credit bureaus as paying multiple bills on time each month, rapidly building your business credit score.
2. Keep your utilization rate low. Just like with personal credit, it's a good idea to charge less than 20% or 30% of your total credit limit on each line of trade credit

you have. This demonstrates that you have a lot of "wiggle room"—a lot of credit you can take advantage of if an emergency should ever interrupt your business's cash flow.

3. Pay your bill on time each month. Every on-time payment you make counts favorably toward building your credit score, while late payments can quickly harm it. Build your business's cash flow so that full on-time payments are a matter of routine and watch your business credit score grow.

HOW AND WHY TO MONITOR

If you do all the above each month, your credit score should grow steadily and eventually become excellent. However, there are a number of reasons it's useful to monitor your business's credit reports regularly. These include:

- Business credit reports don't *just* report your credit and payment history. As mentioned, some business credit reports also report your overall revenue and cash flow, your business's "family tree" of related businesses, and other factors related to your business. All of these factors can be optimized, and all are important to be aware of when planning to apply for new credit.
- Some of these factors, such as your business's family tree, may also change without your knowledge due to the actions of your business partners or their affiliates, and that is important to be aware of.
- The potential for error. Whether it's a credit bureau reporting something incorrectly, fraud arising from a malicious actor getting access to your company's business credit line, or an error with the submission or processing of your monthly payment, it's a good idea

to monitor your credit reports in case any errors occur that need to be corrected.

- Are you growing fast enough? Factors such as your credit mix (the mix of different types of accounts) can affect how fast your credit grows, so it's worth keeping tabs on how *fast* your credit score is rising to see if its rate of growth is meeting your expectations. If not, you might look at what types of accounts you lack that could speed things up.

So now that you've started to establish business credit, it's a good idea to check at least some of your credit reports on an at-least-quarterly basis. Many services also exist which will notify you daily, weekly, or monthly of any changes to your credit report.

It is also important to know that signing up for a credit monitoring service generally does *not* adversely impact your credit score. While making a "hard inquiry" about your credit in pursuit of opening a new credit line may temporarily hurt your score, routine credit monitoring services do not have the same effect.

Both free and paid credit monitoring services are available. Paid services may have advantages such as increased frequency of alerts, greater accuracy, and may include added features. Fraud, identity theft insurance, and monitoring of the dark web to see if your information has been leaked by hackers are two common services offered by paid credit monitoring services.

For my money, if you can pay a few dollars per month for tens or hundreds of thousands of dollars in identity theft insurance, that's a good investment.

So which credit reports should you monitor, and why?

DUN & BRADSTREET

As we've discussed, Dun & Bradstreet is a useful report for creditors and business owners because it provides a comprehensive picture of a business's health. Even beyond monitoring for errors and fraud, this is an excellent report to examine if you're looking for ways to improve your business's overall well-being and future prospects.

Once you have established your Dun & Bradstreet report, you will have access to useful pieces of information like:

- Your PAYDEX score. This number from 1 to 100 indicates your level of risk of paying your creditors back late or incompletely. The higher your score, the better Dun & Bradstreet thinks you will be at successfully repaying loans and credit lines on time. Scores over 80 are considered excellent and give you a high chance of obtaining success and low-interest rates when applying for almost any kind of business financing.
- Your delinquency predictor. This is a number from 1-5 which reflects your likelihood of paying a bill very late or not at all. In this case, a lower number is better: a score of 1 indicates a very low chance of delinquency, while a 5 indicates a very high chance of delinquency. Creditors want to be paid back on time, so businesses with a score of 1 are most likely to get access to the largest credit lines with the most favorable interest rates.
- Your financial stress score. This number is designed to predict the risk that your business will go bankrupt or close its doors in the next 12 months.
- The scores range from 1001-1875, with lower scores being better. Dun & Bradstreet will also sort you into a "class" from 1-5, with class 1 having the lowest risk of bankruptcy or closure, while businesses in class 5 have the highest risk.

If you see your business classified in class 4 or 5 on financial stress, it's time to make some serious changes to your business's cash flow before it's too late!

- Your Supplier Evaluation Risk, or SER rating. This number is designed to predict the risk that your business may cease operating or become inactive in the next 12 months. This particular number is used by businesses who may wish to hire your business as a supplier of parts and services to learn how likely your business is to continue supplying parts and services without interruption.
- SER ratings range from 1-9, with 9 representing the highest risk that your business will be unable to reliably supply parts and services, and 1 representing the lowest risk.
- Your Credit Limit Recommendation. This is a dollar amount representing the maximum amount of credit Dun & Bradstreet would recommend that a lender lend you. This may be used to determine the credit limit on your new credit lines, or the size of any loans you may receive.
- Dun & Bradstreet Rating. This is an overall score based on your company's size, industry, financials, and other factors. Higher scores indicate that a company is more likely to be successful in the long-term and is more likely to pay back its creditors.
- D&B Viability Rating. This is a performance rating that predicts the likelihood that a business will file for bankruptcy, cease operations, or close its doors completely within the next 12 months.
- D&B Cyber Risk Rating. This is an evaluation of how likely cyber threats are to interrupt your operations. This is based on factors like your company's degree of data and network security, and the extent to which your company's operations and finances depend on these computer systems to continue functioning.

I know—that's a lot of numbers and ratings! Each one is calculated based on a slightly different set of factors, drawn from Dun & Bradstreet's analyses of business performance over the years.

Different D&B scores are used by different potential business partners for different purposes. Consider which moves your business might be most likely to make in the near future when deciding which scores to consider optimizing.

Will you be seeking a loan or a major credit line in the near future? Then it might be wise to optimize your PAYDEX score, delinquency predictor, and credit limit recommendation. Will you be seeking to be contracted with other businesses to supply parts or services? Then you may wish to research how to optimize your SER rating.

MONITOR BUSINESS EXPERIAN

Experian is one of the major players in both personal and business credit. Although you might recognize it as one of the major bureaus you monitor for your personal credit, its business credit scoring system is quite different.

Once your Experian credit report has been established, you can check it through Experian or through other credit monitoring services. Your Experian credit score will be a number from 1 to 100, with an Experian business credit score of about 75 indicating excellent odds of approval for business financing and favorable terms on items including credit cards, loans, and certain types of insurance.

MONITOR BUSINESS EQUIFAX

Like Experian, Equifax is a major provider of business and personal credit reports. It is considered one of the top three, along with Dun & Bradstreet and Experian. Like Dun & Bradstreet, Equifax provides several numbers to help potential lenders and buyers rate your business's reliability. These include

- Equifax payment index. This measures the total amount of your business's past payments that were made on time. Like Dun & Bradstreet's PAYDEX score, it is measured on a scale from 0-100, with a score of 10 or lower being good.
- To improve this score, ensure that all your business's bills are paid on time and in full every month.
- Equifax credit risk score. This score ranges from 101-992 and attempts to predict how likely it is that your small business will become severely delinquent on payments. A score of 892 or higher is considered good.
- It takes into account variables like your current credit utilization rate, your business size, the number of transactions your business has paid late, and the total age of your business's credit. To improve this score, keep your credit utilization rate low and your payments on time.
- Equifax business failure score. This score ranges from 1,000 to 1,600. Scores near 1,000 indicate a high chance that a business will fail in the near future, while scores near 1,600 indicate a high probability that your business will continue to exist for the foreseeable future. A score of 1,400 or higher is considered good.
- This score considers factors including the amounts of your business's recent debts, credit utilization rate, overall credit age, and delinquent bills. Pay down your debts, lower your credit utilization, and pay any delinquent bills to improve this score!

REQUEST A LEXISNEXIS REPORT

LexisNexis is another major provider of business credit reports. LexisNexis uses AI to search Internet databases for information including credit and legal records. These reports can include more detailed information, including records of such activities as property purchases.

LexisNexis is legally required to provide you with a free copy of your credit report from their files. Unfortunately , it doesn't always like to do so. LexisNexis has been known to occasionally refuse to send people free reports , claiming that they did not provide sufficient verification to prove their identity.

For this reason, it is recommended that you order your Lexis-Nexis report via registered mail, or with a return receipt request, to ensure that your request for your report and your report itself are both safe, secure, and thoroughly documented . It is also recommended that you keep a date stamped copy of your request.

If LexisNexis doesn't want to provide your free report, it may be necessary to cite your copy of your request and your return receipts proving that LexisNexis did receive your request as evidence to push them to send you your report.

LexisNexis will also request the following types of identification to prove that you are yourself and are therefore entitled to a free report on yourself:

- Your government-issued photo ID, such as a driver's license or state ID card.
- A current bank or credit card statement providing proof of your current address.
- Your Social Security Card.

For more information about how to access your LexisNexis report , you can visit the website listed in this footnote and its associated links.1

REQUEST YOUR CHEXSYSTEMS REPORT

ChexSystems is another type of report that most banks and credit unions look at when verifying an individual and a business as a potential account holder.

A ChexSystems report contains information about bank accounts, the history of delinquent accounts, and more. Inaccurate and negative information on these accounts can have a negative impact on your business, as banks, credit unions, and other financial institutions may be reluctant to do business with you.

For this reason, we recommend that business owners request a copy of their individual and business ChexSystems report at least once a year. This protects against errors and surprises that may be costly when applying for a bank loan or making another major financial move. You can request your ChexSystems report using the link in the footnote below.[2]

WHAT TO DO IF YOU SEE A PROBLEM

If a problem appears on your credit report, the correct approach to fix it will depend on the type of problem.

Problems with late payment, cash flow, and other attributes of your business are relatively "easy" to fix by filing a simple dispute. It's also important to optimize your payment history and cash flow, not just to please credit reporting agencies, but because constant improvement to these metrics is good for the overall health of your business.

But what if a negative mark appears on your credit accounts, and it's *not* because of something you or your business has done? What if you suspect fraud, identity theft, or a reporting error?

The first sign of fraud or identity theft is often unauthorized charges on your credit accounts. If you discover charges on your business credit account that you didn't authorize, the first thing to do is to freeze your credit accounts. This freeze will prevent new charges from being made to these accounts, protecting you from any further unauthorized spending.

Some credit lines may allow you to freeze *only* new or unexpected transactions while continuing to allow your routine monthly payments to go through. This can be useful for allowing you to conduct business as usual while protecting against fraud.[3]

Another way to discover fraud, identity theft, or a credit

reporting error is to notice a change on your credit report that does not match your expectations from your payment history.

When this happens, it's a good idea to first check the relevant account to ensure that the credit report doesn't reflect financial activity you didn't know about. A forgotten unpaid bill or a failed autopay can occasionally result in late payments or nonpayment even though you thought your payment history was up-to-date.

If the credit report issue involves blatantly incorrect information or credit accounts that don't even exist as far as you're aware, you may be dealing with identity theft or erroneous reporting. In this case, you will want to file a dispute with the credit bureau to have the incorrect or fraudulent information removed.

Sometimes, filing a dispute successfully is as simple as using the "dispute" feature on the credit monitoring agency's website. Unfortunately, other times the fraudulent or mistaken information *looks* accurate, so the credit bureau may refuse to remove it from your report initially.

When initial attempts to dispute an error on your credit report are rejected, it may be necessary to escalate your dispute using specific legal language to invoke the agency's legal obligations to remove mistakes from your record. This process can be time-consuming and may require specialized knowledge of the legal requirements for credit reporting to obtain success.

If you do find errors in your credit reports, the Fair Credit Reporting Act requires credit reporting agencies to correct these errors. But the agencies may not always respond promptly, or the first time you file a dispute. To be honest, they may try stall tactics, hoping that you give up so they don't have to spend the time and money to sort out what is correct and remove the erroneous information. It may be necessary to go through an escalation process to get errors removed or contact the creditor directly for help in proving your case.

When disputing a mistake on your credit report, compiling a list of supporting documents or witnesses is a good idea. If, for example, the status of one of your accounts is listed incorrectly or, God forbid, your name is spelled wrong, you will want to compile documents which show your proper account status or a birth certificate and Social Security card showing the proper spelling of your name.

You will want to send copies of the supporting documents—not the originals!—to the bureau whose report you are disputing. Keep the originals safe in case additional copies may be needed in the future.

If negative marks appear on your report, but these are *accurate*, you will want to turn your attention to settling your debts. In many cases, it is possible to move delinquent accounts into good standing within a few months through strategic spending and negotiations with your creditors.

Once your accounts are marked as current and in good standing, you can contact the credit bureau with the mistake to ask them to remove the negative marks from your obsolete account status.

If a credit reporting agency refuses to correct errors on your report or update it to reflect account status changes, there are services that can help you get erroneous or fraudulent marks removed from your credit reports successfully. My own business, Major League Credit & Lending, offers such a service. I sincerely hope you will never need to argue with a credit reporting agency about errors they refuse to remove from your report. But if you ever do, we can help.

If you have handled the dispute process to the fullest extent and appropriate changes still have not been made, you can file a complaint with the Consumer Financial Protection Bureau.[4] This is the primary organization in charge of ensuring that laws to protect consumers, including laws about accurate credit reporting, are followed.

If that still fails to produce results, as a last resort, you can file a lawsuit for violations of Fair Credit Reporting Act statutes. The National Association of Consumer Advocates may be able to help you find legal representation for such an endeavor.[56]

Let us all hope your credit reports remain error-free and are appropriately updated by credit reporting bureaus. But if this fails to happen for some reason, it's good to know that credit advisors, federal agencies, and advocacy organizations have your back and can enforce requirements and assist you in finding legal representation.

CHAPTER 6

BUILDING TIER 2 CREDIT

Now that you've taken some measures to begin to build your credit score, you will become eligible for more advanced trade accounts. It may take a few months, but once your business credit score begins to climb, you may secure better rewards, better interest rates, and higher credit limits on business tradeline accounts from major retailers.

What I call "Tier 2" credit refers to these more advanced tradelines, which may require some credit history to obtain, but which are largely similar to Tier 1 tradelines. Their higher limits and more complex and flexible terms will be good practice for the larger and more complex forms of financing we'll cover in Tiers 3 and 4.

Tier 2 credit tradelines should not require a personal guarantee to back up your line of credit, but they may offer the option of using one. In other words, they may ask whether you, as the business owner, would like to stake your personal credit score or some of your belongings on your promise to pay your invoices.

Giving a personal guarantee is not necessarily bad if you are 100% confident that you will buy no more from this creditor than you can afford to pay back. When using Tier 2 credit primarily to build business credit in order to work toward eventually obtaining bank loans and investors, the hope is that you would be planning to pay off 100% of your business purchases made on credit.

The idea here is not to accumulate too many hard inquiries early on or use credit to buy things you don't already have money for: the idea is to use credit to show that you can establish leverage and responsibly pay off loans so that you can be eligible for much more credit in the future.

So if you are completely sure that you will spend no more than you can easily pay back on a trade line, giving a personal guarantee may be fine. But if you feel any uncertainty about whether your business will be able to continue paying all its bills, or whether someone else in your business might use this tradeline irresponsibly, stick to credit tradelines that do not require a personal guarantee. You don't want to put your personal credit score or assets at risk if you feel any uncertainty about your business's ability to pay all its bills in the next year or so.

When applying for Tier 2 business credit, you will likely be asked for some or all of the following information to allow the vendors to research and verify your business:

- Documentation showing that your business is an entity in legal good standing with your Secretary of State.
- Your Employer Identification Number
- Your business address. This must match on all documents, so if you have more than one address, such as a mailing address and a physical address, choose one to use for your credit applications and stick with it!
- Your D-U-N-S number (this is why we had you apply for this a few months ago.)
- Proof of any licenses your business is required to have in your city and state.

- The information for your separate, dedicated business bank account.
- The phone number under which your business is listed in the 411 directory.

For this chapter, we will focus on vendors that have two attributes which are ideal for businesses seeking to build Tier 2 credit history rapidly. These three important attributes are:

1. Net 30 accounts. While some businesses prefer longer payment periods, Net 30 accounts are the fastest way to build credit history as they report your successful payments to credit bureaus just 30 days after they issue your invoice.
2. Reporting to at least two of the three major business credit reporting agencies. All the vendors we will recommend here report your successful payments to at least two of the following: Dun & Bradstreet, Equifax, and Experian.
3. All of these vendors allow you to pay their invoices with credit cards, including your Brex card. This allows you to have each of your successful payments reported to all three major credit bureaus, and even have your successful payments reported to some of them *twice*.

Any vendor that meets all three above requirements will allow you to rapidly build Tier 2 credit history and rapidly build toward being approved for a bank loan or obtaining investors or other high-caliber business financing options. I've assembled some examples of vendors we know to meet these requirements in this book.

Amazon.com offers business tradeline accounts which allow businesses to take advantage of special wholesale pricing. These accounts do not require a personal guarantee from the business owner.

Amazon reports successful payments made to its business tradeline accounts to Dun & Bradstreet and to Equifax. This means that by making purchases through an Amazon business tradeline and paying your invoice using your Brex secured credit card, your business purchases are being reported to Equifax, Experian, and to Dun & Bradstreet *twice*. Talk about building business credit history!

Lowe's is another vendor that can be useful for businesses in certain industries. Lowe's reports to Equifax, Experian, and Dun & Bradstreet, meaning that if you pay your Lowe's invoice using a Brex credit card, your successful payment will be reported to Equifax once and to Experian and Dun & Bradstreet both twice. Now that's efficient.

Another example of a useful vendor is TigerDirect Electronics. Like Amazon business tradelines, business tradelines from TigerDirect offer special wholesale pricing on electronics that you may need for your business.

TigerDirect reports its payment history to Experian and Equifax, so when you pay your TigerDirect invoices with your Brex credit card, your payment history will be reported to Experian twice in addition to reporting to Equifax and D & B.

These are, of course, just examples of businesses offering Tier 2 business credit tradelines. Countless major retailers and suppliers offer credit tradelines to businesses that have some credit history.

To optimize your business's credit reports, choose vendors that report to at least two: Equifax, Experian, Dun & Bradstreet. Then pay your invoices to these vendors using your Brex credit card to stack your credit reporting history.[1]

Your business is now really building its credit history! With a few months' worth of payments to at least three Tier 1 vendors or credit-building resources under your belt, you're about to level up to adopt a Brex account and credit card and at least three Tier 2 vendors. We will now give all these accounts time to report to the bureaus, which can take up to 90 days.

I have never seen reporting take more than two months, but it's best not to plan anything absolutely requiring that credit reporting occur until 90 days have elapsed. This is another reason to closely monitor your business credit reports.

After these accounts are visibly reporting, it's time to build additional payment history by moving on to the next exciting step: applying for more advanced types of financing!

CHAPTER 7
TIER 3: REVOLVING &
FLEET CREDIT CARDS

Now that you have credit history including Tier 1 and Tier 2 tradelines, we will move on to some truly advanced business credit.

Before applying for these Tier 3 business credit lines, you are going to want to have the following Tier 1 and Tier 2 tradelines to show a truly stellar credit history:

- 7 or more tradelines which report to Dun & Bradstreet. Remember, this can include your Tier 1 and Tier 2 tradelines. If you do not have at least six lines of business credit reporting to Dun & Bradstreet, you may wish to open more and allow one or two invoicing periods to pass before continuing to apply for Tier 3 credit.
- 3 or more tradelines which report to Experian.
- 3 or more tradelines which report to Equifax.
- At least one tradeline with a credit limit greater than $500.

I also recommend that you check your credit reports again if you have not already procured comprehensive credit-monitoring services. As with the last time you "leveled up," you want to know about any potential problems on your reports *before* you apply for these Tier 3 credit lines. Keep an eye out for any surprising or negative information and familiarize yourself with your business's current credit reports. Again, I highly recommend monitoring your business reports through Nav.com.

Once you're familiar with your reports and have taken action to correct any issues that may harm your business's image in the eyes of creditors, let's talk about Tier 3 credit.

In this chapter, we will discuss two kinds of Tier 3 credit.

- Tier 3 credit tradelines. These may offer big benefits to your business, but may not be as helpful to building your credit history as your Tier 1 and Tier 2 tradelines.

TIER 3 CREDIT TRADELINES

Tier 3 credit includes access to tradelines that are valuable for their own sake. Companies that may not offer credit accounts to new businesses without much credit history may offer significant benefits such as wholesale prices and rewards points to more established businesses that have thoroughly proven their ability to pay their invoices reliably.

These tradelines can offer massive value to your business if they improve your access to products your business may need. Some examples of major retailers who offer business credit tradelines to established businesses but not to businesses with little credit history include industry-specific hardware retailers such as flooring and auto parts suppliers, Sam's, Costco, United Airlines, Apple, Best Buy, and a large number of banks and credit unions that offer financial products including retirement portfolios and high-limit credit cards.

While these products may benefit your business, be aware that many of these Tier 3 credit vendors may NOT report your successful payments to them to credit reporting agencies. So take advantage of these elite credit lines if they benefit your business directly, but be aware that you may find that many of these do not help you directly build credit history on your credit report as they do not report to the credit bureaus.

These tier 3 credit vendors can, however, help with your credit history in two ways:

- If you pay your invoices using a business credit card that *does* report to major bureaus, such as your Brex card, you can still have your successful payments to these vendors reported through your credit card company's reporting.
- These credit lines can still act as "trade references." They will not show up on your public credit report if they don't report to the bureaus, so they will not help you qualify for loans or additional credit at first glance when your financier is accessing your public credit reports to decide whether to speak with you further. But if a bank or other financier decides you look promising enough to speak to, you may be given the opportunity to provide evidence of additional "trade references," at which point you can introduce these Tier 3 tradelines as additional evidence that your business is thriving and paying all its bills on time.

Moving up to Tier 3 credit offers some exciting possibilities as far as the types of tradelines you are eligible for and the purchasing power these can give your business. You are now well on your way to having access to tens of thousands of dollars in business financing, all with favorable terms like low-interest rates and long repayment periods!

CHAPTER 8

TIER 4: HIGH-LIMIT CASH LINES OF
CREDIT & MORE FLEET CREDIT

There are many echelons of business credit, from those occupied by the mega-corporations of the world to the Tier 1 credit used by new business owners who are just learning the ropes of busi-ness finance. In this book, we will move up through Tier 4, as this is the gateway into the level of financing at which rapid expansion into a franchise or large corporation can occur if you want it to.

Tier 4 credit includes a number of types of credit that are not typically available to new businesses and businesses without much-reported credit history. These include:

Computer leases from major tech companies.
- Car financing from major car companies.
- Bank credit cards which may have very high credit
- limits, useful rewards programs, and other favorable terms.
Financing from investors who may infuse large
- amounts of cash into your business and may also offer guidance in growing your business to the next level.

Even if you do not plan to seek investors, I recommend that you read this chapter to the end. This is because the questions investors ask can help businesses discover new ideas with the potential for massive business growth even without investors. After all, it is the investors' job to think about how companies can grow. Just like when making your business plan, considering how you would pitch your company to a venture capitalist if you absolutely *had* to get investors to keep your business going may force you to identify opportunities for growth via new inventions, product lines, or business models.

There are many ways you can explore the business credit lines offered by major tech companies, car companies, and other industry-specific vendors. For this chapter, we will focus on information that can be used by almost any business, such as advanced business credit cards and procuring investors.

Before applying for Tier 4 credit lines or pitching to investors, you will want to ensure that you have at least 14 business credit tradelines. These include your 7+ Tier 1 and Tier 2 credit-reporting lines, and any Tier 3 credit lines you may have opened, such as loans or non-reporting trade references.

While juggling 14 accounts may sound like a lot, remember that at this point, most of your business's operating supplies can likely be procured through business credit tradelines and that business credit cards you use to pay your vendor invoices also count as credit lines. If you split your monthly invoices between three or four business credit cards that all report to credit bureaus, for example, those will count as business tradelines on your credit reports without requiring you to buy more things or spend more money.

You are essentially paying for the same purchases twice, and having your purchases count as two separate payment experiences, by first buying from vendors and then paying your vendor invoices with a credit card which you then proceed to pay off in full each month.

If you don't yet have 14 business credit tradelines at this point, take some time to strategize how you might open more tradelines without increasing your cost or administrative burden too much. Is there a way you could use new tradelines to earn more rewards, or open a new business credit card that reports to multiple major credit bureaus and use that to pay some of your existing invoices?

Remember that this process of building credit is also a process of building your organizational and administrative skills. These are essential skills to making strategic decisions for a growing business, and they will serve you well if you choose to undertake massive business growth in the future!

I also recommend that you check your business credit reports before applying for Tier 4 credit or pitching to investors. It's always wise to make sure that there are no unforeseen developments you need to address before making a major financial move that requires your business to undergo the scrutiny of lenders and investors.

Because you are now entering a stage in your business development in which very large amounts of money, debt, and equity may be involved, I have one more warning before you proceed.

GET A LAWYER. NOW.

You must have any agreements with lenders or investors reviewed by a business attorney with whom you have a good relationship before you sign them.

I will say that again: this is *imperative*.

Many business owners go without a business lawyer in the earlier stages of their business to save money. Then, if they don't encounter problems as a result, they may be reluctant to begin paying a lawyer as they take on progressively more complex and high-stakes business agreements.

However, you must have an attorney look over any agreements with investors, and the more money you invest into borrowing through other forms of financing, the higher the stakes will be. This is the ownership and control over your business we are talking about here. It is not unheard of for unscrupulous investors and/or clueless business owners to create a situation where the investor has taken a large degree of ownership and control of a company without the business owner realizing it.

It is preferable to develop an ongoing relationship with a business lawyer whom you trust at this stage. If you are looking at potentially obtaining credit cards with $100,000 monthly credit limits, you have the necessary cash flow to warrant this.

Such lawyers may be helpful in looking over *all* contracts that your business uses or signs, since the more success your business has, the more money it may have to lose in the event of lawsuits or simply bad contracts which sign away too many rights.

So find a business lawyer that you trust *now* if you haven't already. It's time to make a good lawyer part of your business family.

TIER 4 BUSINESS CREDIT CARDS

Tier 4 business credit cards are designed for established businesses. This is why they aren't typically available to new businesses with extensive credit histories proving their ability to manage cash flow and pay their bills.

Once your business has sufficiently proven its financial prowess by building up credit history, you will become eligible for Tier 4 credit cards and other credit lines from companies such as:

- Frost Bank offers business credit cards with no annual fees and monthly credit limits of up to $100,000.
- American Express Corporate offers cards for businesses with less than $4 million in annual revenue which accrue rewards points that can be used with airlines and which, in some cases, may have *no* credit limit.
- Citizens Bank offers business credit cards with no annual fee and options to choose between low-interest rates and high reward points programs.

These are, of course, just a few examples of the top recommended business credit cards available to a business with Tier 4 credit. It is likely that nearly every bank and credit union offers some kind of elite business credit card. Some may require that your business have several million dollars in annual revenue in addition to a stellar credit score, but others may have options specifically for small business owners.

If these business credit cards sound interesting to you, now is the point where you may be well-qualified to apply for them. Take some time to research business credit card options offered by your local banks, or those which offer industry-specific discounts and rewards points that you may be able to use to cut your business's operating costs.

It's also time to consider whether you want to seek investors for your business. While investment capital can be a powerful tool for fueling massive business growth, keep in mind that investors may also ask for some control over company operations decisions, which may not be necessary for every business.

APPLY FOR A BREX BUSINESS ACCOUNT

Now that your business has some credit history from using the strategies discussed in our Tier 1 chapter, you may qualify for a Brex business account. A Brex account is similar to a bank account but is superior to a typical checking account in several ways.

Brex accounts are insured by the FDIC just like bank accounts are, but money held in Brex accounts can be sent via ACH or wired worldwide for free. Brex accounts also allow unlimited users and cards to be linked to your account, offer business rewards programs, and count toward your business credit history.

Brex can't replace your business bank account, but it can be an extremely useful tool if you want to build business credit history or make it easier to move money internationally, or make funds available to multiple members of your business.

Just remember that with great power comes great responsibility: if you are going to move money internationally or make it available to more members of your businesses, make sure to keep close tabs on that spending to ensure you will be able to pay all your invoices in full at the end of the month.

Once you have a Brex account, you will receive a Brex business card. This card is secured by the money you have in your Brex account, but it functions otherwise like a credit card. Brex reports your successful (or unsuccessful) payments on this credit card to Experian and Dun & Bradstreet.

I recommend that you use this card to make your invoice payments moving forward. In a way, this allows you to count your payment history toward your business credit history twice: once when you pay the vendors, and again when you pay Brex to cover those expenses.

Once you have built even more credit history by maintaining Tier 1-3 vendor accounts and paying off a secured Brex credit card for a few months, you will eventually qualify for an *unsecured* Brex credit card, which offers a higher limit and more rewards that your business can use. An unsecured Brex credit card represents tremendous purchasing power; by the time you get there, you will have cultivated the necessary skills to use it responsibly!

SEEKING INVESTORS

There are several tiers of investing, just as there are many tiers of business credit. When you investigate an established company's investors profile, you may find information saying that it has been through various "rounds" of financing. This can refer to investing from different types of investors who have specific business models for investing at companies in different stages of development.

As you will see from this section, getting investors can be quite a competitive and specialized endeavor. It can be even more challenging than getting a bank loan since investors are hoping that you will not merely manage to pay them back, but that your business will grow so much that the money they invest with you will be multiplied. I plan to release a whole book on the topic of how to get investors —and avoid signing bad investment agreements—in 2024.

For now, I wanted to include an overview of the process of getting investors here to demystify this process and give you an idea of what to expect and what to research further if your business decides to seek investors as a form of financing.

The first tier of investing for most businesses is called "angel investing." These are the investors who are most willing to invest in new businesses that have not previously worked with investors and who may be new to the business world altogether.

After you have finished reading this chapter, completed the recommended exercises, and compiled the recommended materials, you can begin to search for angel investors through the following organizations:

- Angel Capital Association
- Angel Investment Network
- Gust (formerly known as AngelSoft)

The second tier of investment for many businesses is called " venture capital funding ." The name kind of says it all. Venture capitalists specialize in investing in new and relatively unproven businesses in hopes of "getting on the ground floor of the next big thing." The "venture" in "venture capital" refers to the fact that this is considered a little bit riskier and more uncertain than other types of investing, as we see below:

Venture:

Noun: A risky or daring journey or undertaking.

Verb: To dare to do something or go somewhere that may be dangerous or unpleasant.

—Oxford Languages

It is possible to obtain venture capital without first having obtained angel investors, although it can be more challenging.

Because angel investors and venture capital funds often seek similar things in the businesses they invest in, we will combine their requirements into a single section for the purposes of this book.

A venture capitalist's hope is that the company they invest in grows to become very large, and their investment's value will thus be multiplied. Imagine, for example, being one of the first investors in Apple. As a venture capitalist investing in Apple, you could have purchased a large number of Apple shares for a fraction of the current share price. You could have ended up owning a large chunk of the company for what would be a tiny investment compared to Apple's worth today.

Because venture capitalists choose businesses that are newer and less proven, they will want rigorous information about your company's past growth and plans for the future to convince them that you have the potential to grow by orders of magnitude in the years to come. Only then will they give you a large infusion of cash in exchange for partial ownership of your company.

Venture capital funds will also often serve as "fund managers," signaling to other investors that they believe in this company and inviting other investors to invest. They often charge an annual fee for managing the company's investment fund for a period of 7 to 10 years, during which they hope the company will establish rapid growth.

Because they will then have invested a great deal of their own money into your company's success, venture capitalists will also have an interest in providing guidance to optimize your company's chances of massive growth.

This may be very desired if you are a financially motivated business owner who wants your company to become as big as possible. On the other hand, it may be very undesired if you are a craft-driven business owner who wants to ensure that certain business practices or quality standards are adhered to, even if these may not be compatible with rapid growth into a large corporation.

This is why it's a good idea to carefully consider what your real goals are for your business. Some business owners are motivated by building as much personal and generational wealth as possible; others are motivated by something else entirely.

After a company is already fairly large and successful, investments from other types of entities become more likely. Many different types of investors exist who seek to invest in companies at different stages of their growth and in different situations. Larger businesses or business owners may seek to buy your company from you for a large amount of money, or to buy a stake in your company as a first step toward acquisition. Businesses whose cash flow and growth have stabilized may even " go public" and be traded on the stock market where the general public can invest by buying shares.

If you decide you want to seek investments and guidance from venture capitalists, how do you demonstrate to these investors that your business is an excellent prospect to invest in?

Venture capital companies look for companies with big potential for high ROI—return on investment—within a defined "investment horizon," or time limit, such as the 7-10 years mentioned above. This means that venture capitalists will be interested in many of the items you compiled for your business plan and financial projections when applying for a loan. They will want to know things like how you will use their money, what ROI you expect on that money, and how much you see your company's total cash flow and value growth over the next 7-10 years if you receive this funding.

Unlike most lenders, venture capitalists may also want the right and responsibility of seeking out opportunities for financial and business growth that you haven't spotted yet, such as new business practices, target audiences, marketing practices, or technologies. This is a valuable service for growth-minded business owners, but following these recommendations may also become a requirement after a venture capital fund has invested in your business.

The following is a list of things that angel investors and venture capitalists look for in their companies. Following these best practices may help optimize your business's chances of success and growth, even if you don't seek investors since these items are designed to assure venture capitalists that your business will grow wildly in the years to come.

#1: DISRUPTIVE POTENTIAL

Venture capitalists tend to particularly want to hear about your business's "disruptive" potential. In this case, "disruption" refers to your business having a business model, method, or technology that is so unique that it has the potential to "disrupt" the way business is currently done in your industry. This is why most venture capitalists are active in the tech space, where new technologies often fundamentally change the way we go about our everyday lives. But other new inventions, methods, or business models may also fit the bill for "disruptive" potential.

Companies with advantages when seeking venture capital include:

- Those that have invented a new technology which has capabilities other technologies don't have.
- Those whose products are markedly different from the competition or offer features not found in any other product.
- Disruptive business models, such as those that offer significant advantages over existing mainstream business models in operating costs or customer experience.

Some business owners who seek venture capital funding may feel that they do not have the potential to achieve it. If, for example, their business is not a tech business. Venture capital requirements can also spur business owners to think outside the box and discover ideas with potential for explosive growth. These attributes describe businesses that have the potential to rapidly outpace their competition through innovation and can create the potential for greater growth with or without venture capital funding.

#2 THE RIGHT TEAM

We've mentioned a few times throughout this book how important it is to have the right leadership team for business success. We've talked about how having business partners with less than sterling reputations can become a problem for your business's "family tree" in your Dun & Bradstreet report. Your business partners must be extremely trustworthy to be trusted with your business's money, and credit, and your team's expertise and experience are key to convincing lenders that your business will succeed and pay back the money they loan you with interest.

Venture capitalists take this to the next level. They know that the success of a business is more about the people running the business than about the business's ideas or technologies. Are the people in charge hard-working and dedicated to success? Do they have the emotional temperament to work together through the ups and downs of a new business and provide a positive experience for their business partners? Can they analyze their business's finances and make strategic business decisions to optimize growth?

Venture capital firms will want to see that your team has good ideas, technical expertise, emotional intelligence, and a track record of good decision-making. This doesn't mean you all have to be perfectly prim and proper; often, people with a bit of a risk-taking streak do best in business. But you will want a team that demonstrates a commitment to the success of your business, an ability and willingness to make strategic decisions and change course as needed, and the emotional resilience to handle conflicts and crises that might arise during the course of a young business's life.

Venture capitalists will look for these things—but they are also things that any business can benefit from.

Now is a good time to analyze your leadership team honestly

and look for any weak points in these areas. Are there points that could be improved upon? Is there some kind of training or coaching you or your business partners could procure to make you better executives who are best suited to take the actions necessary to grow your business?

#3 THE RIGHT MARKET

One major indicator of a business's likely future success is the general market demand for its product. If you are in a business selling products that have been rendered obsolete by a new invention, for example, you had better innovate your product offerings fast! On the other hand, if you are selling a product or service that is rapidly growing in popularity, you are likely to experience growth even if you are not one of the most stream-lined players in that industry.

As such, venture capitalists will want to see numbers regarding your overall target market. "Target market" encompasses both your industry—the market for the specific type of good or service you provide—and demand for your good or service within a specific target demographic if you have one.

If, for example, you are particularly good at solving a problem that affects mostly people of a certain socioeconomic background, educational background, or cultural background, that could give you an advantage or disadvantage depending on whom your product or service is specialized for.

Can you find numbers to indicate whether demand for your product or service is currently rising or falling? Are there specific groups of people among whom the demand is rising? If demand for your product or service is falling, is there a way you can pivot to provide products and services that meet the changing demands of the market?

Venture capitalists will want to see the most specific numbers possible regarding the demand for your product in today's market. And you will want to see these numbers as a business owner, as they will help you plan for the years ahead.

#4 SALES

Generally, venture capitalists will want to see that you already have a track record of steadily growing sales over the lifespan of your company. The more sales growth you're able to demonstrate, the more likely venture capitalists are to believe that more growth is very likely in your future.

Have you been able to demonstrate growth in sales? If not, how can you prioritize that right now? What are the missing parts of your sales or marketing process that are preventing sales growth?

Even if you are not seeking to procure venture capitalist funding, buckling down and learning how to grow sales is an important growth step for you as a business owner.

#5 FINANCIAL PLAN

This financial plan has many things in common with the business plan we discussed when applying for business loans. Venture capitalists will want to see how you plan to allocate your current funds and your investment funds to areas like:

- Advertising
- Expansion
- Acquisition of new resources
- Outsourcing non-core functions to optimize your results and your revenue.

Seeing how exactly you plan to allocate funds to these areas gives venture capitalists a good idea of your likelihood of success. Putting together such a plan, including using any current numbers available for costs, revenue, and ROI for each component of your business's operations, can help you grow your business massively with or without investment funding.

#6 FUTURE PROJECTIONS

Venture capital funds will want to see detailed breakdowns of your costs and profits from your business's years to date and detailed projections of what you can reasonably expect your finances to look like in future years.[1]

Use the specifics you put together for your financial plan to project in detail exactly how much growth you can reasonably expect to see based on your costs, revenue, and ROI details in combination with your plans for spending investment capital.

The result should be a solid plan for turning investment capital—or any other kind of capital you receive, such as loans, credit lines, and your own growing revenue—into larger and larger profits each year.

You may or may not choose to pursue investors for your business. But either way, you can learn a lot about streamlining your business for growth and how innovation can help you to grow by answering the questions investors ask when considering whether to invest in a business.

I hope that this chapter leaves you with renewed insight into how your brand can innovate, change, and grow with changing times, as well as increased purchasing power!

CHAPTER 9
BUSINESS LOANS

We've now seen how building business credit can create some truly impressive financing options. But what about that often-discussed holy grail of small business owners, the business loan?

KNOW YOUR LOAN OPTIONS

So far in this book, we have focused on what credit bureaus call "revolving tradelines." These are tradelines whose value turns over, or "revolves" on a regular basis. Credit lines where you make purchases on credit and then pay off those purchases on a regular basis are revolving tradelines.

Loans and mortgages, on the other hand, are "installment tradelines." This refers to the fact that, instead of borrowing money and paying it back in a revolving fashion, you borrow one large amount of money and then pay it back in installments over the course of months or years.

Successfully paying off a loan for years to come requires a certain level of financial stability, foresight, and planning, which is why installment tradelines like loans and mortgages are typically difficult to get approved for unless you already have spectacular credit history and cash flow. This is also why most new business owners who apply for a loan while their business is still in its infancy are denied: lenders simply don't have the confidence that they have the skill and cash flow necessary to pay off a loan that may total tens or hundreds of thousands of dollars.

The good news is you now have the skills and the credit history of making this happen. If you have successfully been paying off seven or more Tier 1 and Tier 2 tradelines for four to six months, you have both demonstrated reliability and developed the planning and cash management skills necessary to add installment payments on a loan to your business' list of monthly bills.

If you want a large infusion of cash in the form of a business loan, you now have sufficient credit history that lack of credit history is not likely to be an obstacle when you apply.

However, as you will see in this section, many types of loans exist, and different types may be right for different businesses. In addition, applying for loans is a very competitive process, and there is a science to impressing different kinds of lenders. Having a stellar business credit report is almost always essential to obtain a good loan, but other aspects of your loan application will also be important. I plan to release an entire book to cover this subject in more depth later in 2023, so stay tuned for details.

For now, I wanted to include an overview of the process of applying for loans to give you an idea of the basic types available and the basic steps involved. If you feel that applying for a loan for you is right now, you can seek out my book or other resources to learn more details about what to look for in a great loan for your business model and how exactly to wow a loan officer.

Many types of small business loans exist. When comparing the options available to you, consider questions like:

- Why do you need the funding? How will you use it to increase your profit to the point that it's easy to pay back the loan while building massive wealth on top of the repayment cost?

- How fast do you need the money? Some types of loans take longer to approve than others, and larger loans are often slower to be approved.
- How much money do you really need? Will you benefit more from a $500,000 investment, or will $50,000 get the job done and allow your business to level up?
- What will be the total cost of debt if you take this loan? Consider factors like interest rates and any penalties for early repayment (some banks will charge fees if you repay your loan early because the interest that accrues over time is their source of profit). A good accountant or financial advisor may be helpful to you when analyzing these questions.

Several types of business loans are available that you may wish to investigate. These include:

- Bank loans. These can range in size from $10,000 to $1,000,000. They can be more challenging to get than some types of loans, but they also tend to have lower interest rates than loans that are easier to obtain, so if you get approved you will likely save money over time.
- Small Business Administration loans. The Small Business Administration is an agency run by the federal government with the mission of helping small businesses to grow and thrive. The approval process for SBA loans can be slow, but they offer a wide range of interest rates from low to high and can offer longer repayment terms than other loan types meaning you will have longer to pay back the money. They can range in size from $30,000 to $5,000,000.
- Business term loans. These may be offered by online lenders, and range in size from $100 to $500,000. They typically have shorter repayment terms, which is good

if you want to get debt off your plate quickly, but not so great if you'd rather have a longer time to repay. They can also have higher interest rates than other loan types, so read the terms carefully. They may be best to use for one-time purchases such as equipment. However, there is also…

- Equipment financing. This is a form of financing specifically for buying equipment for your business. It is a bit like a lease in that the lender agrees to pay for some or all of the cost of your equipment and its installation, and you repay them gradually over time. However, if you cannot make your payments, the lender can repossess your equipment. These loans can have lower interest rates than business-term loans, but are obviously less flexible in how they can be used.

Which type of funding sounds best to you?

Would you rather go through a slow approval process for the chance at lower interest rates, or do you want to be assured of having money soon? Do you want to borrow a large amount to purchase a property or buy a large expansion for your equipment or staff, or would you rather have a smaller loan to pay for modest growth? Would you like to have many years to pay off a big loan, or would you like to get the debt off your plate quickly with a term loan? Would equipment financing help you to grow while minimizing the amount you need to repay?

Once you have decided what types of business loans look best to you, the next step is applying. This is a time to be strategic, because applying for a business loan may constitute a "hard inquiry" which can temporarily take points off your credit score. Therefore, it's a good idea to identify the two or three loans that seem best to you. I recommend starting by applying to your favorite first when your credit score is best, and sending out subsequent applications one at a time if your first application does not succeed.

It is also good to seek lenders like those recommended by my company, Major League Credit & Lending, who offer pre-approvals first and will not cost a hard inquiry until you accept the loan agreement. You can avoid many hard inquiries by getting pre-approved for financing. In some cases, having your bank's pre-approval for financing may even allow you to obtain other types of credit lines without them feeling the need to send a hard inquiry since they already have your bank's promise to finance you and most likely a recent credit report.

When you have zeroed in on your favorite loan options, you will probably find information about what your business needs to qualify for these loans successfully. Look for information like:

- What business credit scores are preferred or required.
- Whether the lender prefers or requires that your business has operated for a certain period of time. Some will require several years of successful business history before making a large loan.
- Does the lender prefer or require a certain amount of cash flow from a business? Some may prefer to only give large loans to businesses who already have seven-figure annual cash flows.
- Does the loan require collateral, such as a personal guarantee or security through assets? If so, decide how comfortable you are with this. Are you confident enough that the funding will allow you to build wealth, or would you prefer to keep your personal credit score and assets protected?

Now that you've researched your options, it's a good idea to make sure your business plan is in ship shape.

Have you learned what is most profitable for your business model and warrants changes to your business plan? Have there been changes to items such as your leadership team, your marketing plan, or your financials since you first wrote your business plan?

This is a good time to revisit the section on business plans toward the end of Chapter 2. If you have been following our six-month plan, you may have learned a lot about what does and doesn't work to make your business profitable by now. You may also have expanded your cash flow using the credit lines you've acquired over the last four months. Your newly gained experience and knowledge will help you make the most impressive possible business plan to show to lenders.

Use this as an opportunity to optimize your business finances and operations as well. You may realize something while updating your business plan that could help you to make more money if implemented across your company.

Once your business plan is up-to-date and looks great, you will also want to create a funding request for your potential lenders. Explain how much funding you are asking for and why. Do you want debt or equity, and why have you made that choice? What repayment term would you like, and why? What will you do with the loan money?

If possible, use your funding request to break down a budget for how you will spend the loan money and cite any numbers that lead you to believe you will get a positive return on investment.

Consider questions like how much revenue an average employee, store location, or piece of equipment generates for you if you plan to use loan money to pay for these. Consider questions like what kind of ROI your history and research suggests you can get from the marketing campaign you have planned if you plan to use the funding to do marketing. The more specific numbers and details you can cite to convince lenders that you will make a positive return on investment for the loan money you spend, the more likely they will be to grant your loan.

You may also wish to include financial projections in your business plan and/or funding request. Include income statements, balance sheets, and cash flow statements from your business's past five years (if your business has been around that long). Include projections for how you expect these numbers to change over time if you are able to secure loan money and subsequently pay for additional employees, locations, equipment, marketing, etc.

You can download some examples from the Small Business Administration's website, or by visiting the link in this footnote.[1]

Your business plan is an excellent place to consolidate information for your potential lender, and it will also help you gain insight into the possible ways your business can grow. Once you have assembled your business plan, you will also want to gather…

YOUR LONG-TERM BUSINESS GOALS

In addition to your business plan, your potential lender will want to hear about your long-term business goals. This is important because there are several strategies business owners use when seeking to make a living or a profit off of a business.

Some business owners start their business because they just love providing that product or service. Such a business owner may wish to remain in control of their company until they retire. This will affect whether they want to seek investors who may bring financing and expertise to the business, but who may also desire some control over business decisions and decisions about daily operations. Such a business owner may want to plan to sell the company to another business owner at a large profit when they retire or may wish to pass on leadership to a trusted friend or family member, which means training a family member or other protégé instead of preparing the company to be sold.

Other business owners may be very financially minded. They may seek to profit financially as much as possible, as quickly as possible. This can mean putting the business on a fast track to attract investors or being sold to another company for a large sum. Existing companies will often buy highly profitable small businesses from their owners for large sums since they are essentially purchasing the company's profits for years to come. Some entrepreneurs even make a business model out of repeatedly starting companies and then selling them to larger companies when they have become highly successful.

Insomnia Cookies is an example of a company which was founded less than twenty years ago as a cookie delivery service based out of a student's dorm room and is now a huge national chain that its founders sold to Krispy Kreme. We don't know how much Krispy Kreme paid for the controlling stake in Insomnia Cookies, but it's a safe bet that it was at least in the millions.

None of these types of success happen without strategic planning. This is why it is essential to know your long-term goal. When you retire, do you want to sell your company for millions of dollars? Do you want that to be ten years from now or fifty years from now? Is it more important to you to keep the company in the family as a form of generational wealth, or to make sure that it's run in the right way, such that you may wish to retain ownership or pass ownership to a trusted individual? If you are more focused on making money than controlling your company's operations, do you want to attract investors?

What are the best practices followed by business owners who have found success in achieving their personal long-term goals for their business?

Being able to articulate your long-term vision for your company and why you have chosen that vision will tell your potential lenders that you are thinking strategically and will make strategic financial decisions—including the necessary decisions to pay them back!

TIME TO APPLY

When applying for your dream loan, be sure to read the requirements to determine what documents you will need.

Having your business plan and long-term business goal in mind is always a good idea, but different lenders may also require you to bring tax returns, cash flow sheets, business licenses, proof of patents or copyrights, and other legal documents to verify the information on your business plan and to prove that you are in good legal standing with all relevant government authorities.[2]

Read the requirements of each individual loan and lender and be sure to also take note of such specific details as their expected turnaround time. Some types of loans may grant approval within days or even minutes, while others may take weeks or months to get back to you. Don't assume that a faster turnaround time is better; those who take longer may do so because they are evaluating many competing businesses which all want their favorable loan terms.

WHAT DO YOU CHOOSE?

Now that you have an established business credit history, you can make big decisions about your company's future. Do you want to expand and build wealth as quickly as possible, or dedicate your attention to your craft and community? Do you want a big business loan to enable rapid expansion, or do you want to keep your installment payments low? Do you want to sell your company for millions of dollars someday, or keep it all in the family?

The sky is the limit when you make strategic business decisions. The truth is, everyone can run a business that is capable of massive growth; it is just a matter of asking the right questions and making strategic decisions.

As you can see from this chapter so far, applying for business loans can be quite a complex undertaking, so I'm working on an upcoming book about the subject which will cover topics like different types of loans available to you, red flags, and green flags to look for before signing a loan agreement, and optimizing your application to make the most robust possible case to your lender for why your business is an excellent candidate to receive this loan. I hope this book will assist those of you who want to move on to this next step of applying for business financing in the form of loans.

CHAPTER 10
GO FORTH AND GROW!

I am honored that you have chosen me to assist you on your business credit journey. This work means so much to me, as it means helping individuals to build personal and generational wealth.

You have now completed a comprehensive crash course on going from not having a business at all to procuring elite business credit lines, business loans, and potentially even investors who can guide you to massive business growth. I hope you can execute as many of these steps as you wish to make your business goals a reality.

Remember that building business credit and procuring financing takes time and perseverance. There is a tried and tested system which has a very high success rate for allowing any business owner to procure large amounts of financing for their business—but procuring success requires following these steps meticulously and in order.

I expect the completion of these steps to take between four months to a year for most business owners. In that time, you will grow tremendously as a business owner and a person.

In filing the necessary paperwork, you will gain fortitude, and the legal protections afforded by incorporating your business and separating its finance and liabilities from your own.

In procuring Tier 1 and Tier 2 business credit, you will grow your organizational and money management skills, and establish your business's credibility as a solid and legitimate corporation as a matter of public record.

In procuring Tier 3 and 4 business credit, you will gain access to vast amounts of business funding and financing—likely more than you now believe is possible. You will also ask advanced questions and assemble advanced cost-benefit analyses and financial projections, which will arm you with the knowledge and mindset you need to create genuinely massive growth for your business if you choose to do so.

If you want your business to remain small and craft-focused, that's okay. But if you want to become a national corporation with multiple locations, that is also within your reach if you follow the best practices listed here and continue to research further into some of the areas we have only briefly addressed.

Everything is within your reach. It's just a matter of combining strategic knowledge of business and finance with hard work and dedication.

That's the lesson I've learned on my own journey from never-run-a-business entrepreneur to founder and owner of multiple businesses. That's the lesson I wanted to share in this book, and it is a lesson that I hope will empower you and your loved ones with the necessary knowledge to take control of your lives.

If you have a moment, it would be very helpful to me and others if you could review this book on Amazon and/or Audible. Your review will help direct others to this book who may benefit from the knowledge it contains.

I wish you the best of luck and am so excited about your journey!

Leave a 1-Click Review!

I would be incredibly thankful if you could take just 60 seconds to write a brief review on Amazon, even if it's just a few sentences!

AFTERWORD

Thank you for taking the time to make it to the end. In conclusion, we've learned a lot about the values of entrepreneurship, business and personal credit, and how you can use them to propel yourself forward no matter your resources or circumstances.

The wealth gap in America has severely separated the poor from the wealthy, not because people lack the ability, but because many lack the information and guidance to measure up. However, following many of the same tactics mentioned in this book, I have been able to overcome hurdles and leverage my creditworthiness, lendability, and knowledge to grow my business and brand - these methods work!

If you are unsure or a bit nervous about the process, again, my company Major League Credit & Lending has a complete business credit-building system that will walk you through each step from A-Z of starting your business and obtaining the startup capital that you need. You can do this without current cash flow, jeopardizing your personal credit, or having collateral. In fact, you are guaranteed to acquire at least $50,000 in funding in the first 6-12 months if you follow the blueprint.

Feel free to explore more information about all the business services I offer on my website at https://majorleaguecr.com/ or schedule a free consultation here https://majorleaguecr.com/business-credit-consultation. On the website, you will learn more about the platform, other business funding options, personal loans, and even consumer financing for your clients or customers.

Peace and blessings,
Chevon

OTHER BOOKS YOU'LL LOVE!

The Credit Game: Plays We Were Never Taught

Retirement Planning Handbook

FREE GIFT FOR READERS

Or Visit: https://www.bit.ly/TCGgift

ABOUT THE AUTHOR

Chevon K. Patrick is a credit educator, and founder and President of Major League Credit Repair, LLC. She established Major League Credit Repair after realizing how much she and her peers had not been taught about credit and finance in school or life. After discovering that good credit is the key to financial literacy, and to multiplying wealth using other people's money, Chevon set out to provide education and expert assistance to others like herself.

Chevon has a particular passion for serving, educating, and investing in Black communities and Black business owners. She has seen how historical injustice and lack of financial education opportunities too often creates a cycle of poverty.

Chevon is also a mother, a cancer survivor, a student, and a believer in spiritual healing. She currently lives with her youngest son Kaelon while admiring the musical talent and career of her older son, Taejon. She is still, unfortunately, grieving the loss of her youngest daughter, Yevaeh, who was nine. It is her profound hope that the soul as well as the entire body of the Black community can be healed and made whole through God, skillful use of financial education, spiritual guidance and whatever else may be necessary to build overall prosperity.

Website: https://majorleaguecr.com/
Consultations: calendly.com/majorleaguecreditrepair

facebook.com/majorleaguecreditrepair
instagram.com/majorleaguecredit

RESOURCES

NAV Business Credit Monitoring https://nav.nkwcmr.net/oejqZ9

FREE Consultation - calendly.com/majorleaguecreditrepair

Personal Credit Dispute Kit

https://drive.google.com/drive/folders/1uOHmqTXWl-ca42CtMusYeeI1omvizPihy?usp=sharing

Opus Virtual Office https://www.opusvirtualoffices.com/aff2/majorleaguecreditrepair/

Regus Virtual Office https://www.myregus.com/

Experian http://www.experian.com

Small Business Administration http://www.sba.gov

Dun & Bradstreet http://www.dnb.com/

Equifax http://www.equifax.com

Free Gift https://bit.ly/TCGgift

Leave a Review https://www.amazon.com/review/create-review/edit?ie=UTF8&channel=glance-detail&asin=B0BDSRQL4M

*may earn commissions

NOTES

INTRODUCTION

1. *5 surprising ways your business is impacted by poor credit: FleetCardsUSA*. Fleet-CardUSA. (n.d.). Retrieved October 7, 2022, from https://fleetcardsusa.com/blog/five-surprising-ways-your-business-is-impacted-by-poor-credit/
2. *10 stats that explain why business credit is important for small business*. U.S. Small Business Administration. (n.d.). Retrieved October 7, 2022, from https://www.sba.gov/blog/10-stats-explain-why-business-credit-important-small-business

1. YOUR BUSINESS CREDIT STRATEGY

1. Anna.Baluch. (2019, October 17). *What is tier 1 credit?* Experian. Retrieved November 4, 2022, from https://www.experian.com/blogs/ask-experian/what-is-tier-1-credit/

2. BUILD YOUR FOUNDATION

1. How to name a business in 5 simple steps (2022). The BigCommerce Blog. (2022, August 24). Retrieved October 7, 2022, from https://www.bigcommerce.com/blog/how-to-name-a-business/
2. Staff, D. (2022, June 28). *Is domain squatting still a factor in 2022? here's the lowdown*. Digital.com. Retrieved October 7, 2022, from https://digital.com/best-domain-registrars/domain-squatting/
3. Drake Forester - June 27, 2019. (2022, May 6). Should you incorporate your business in another state? SCORE. Retrieved October 7, 2022, from https://www.score.org/blog/should-you-incorporate-your-business-another-state
4. *Apply for an employer identification number (EIN) online*. Internal Revenue Service. (n.d.). Retrieved October 8, 2022, from https://www.irs.gov/businesses/small-businesses-self-employed/apply-for-an-employer-identification-number-ein-online
5. McCraw, C., & Guzman, M. D. (2022, March 10). *Google Voice Review: Is it right for your business?* Fit Small Business. Retrieved October 8, 2022, from https://fitsmallbusiness.com/google-voice-review/

3. ESTABLISH (AND FIX!) YOUR BUSINESS CREDIT REPORTS

1. Rashkovich, B. (2020, August 11). *FICO SBSS business credit score: How to understand and improve yours.* Fundera. Retrieved October 20, 2022, from https://www.fundera.com/blog/fico-sbss#sources
2. Rashkovich, B. (2020, August 11). *FICO SBSS business credit score: How to understand and improve yours.* Fundera. Retrieved October 20, 2022, from https://www.fundera.com/blog/fico-sbss#sources

4. BUSINESS CREDIT TIER 1: NET 30 ACCOUNTS

1. "NET Terms Guide: What Are NET 30/60/90 Terms?" Resolve. Accessed December 13, 2022. https://resolvepay.com/blog/post/net-terms/.
2. "Online Home Store for Furniture, Decor, Outdoors & More." Wayfair. Accessed December 13, 2022. https://www.wayfair.com/.
3. "Office Supplies, Cleaning Supplies & More for Every Workspace." Cleaning & Office Supplies for Every Workspace | Quill.com. Accessed December 13, 2022. https://www.quill.com/.
4. "Compare Credit Options - Office Depot." officedepot.com. Accessed December 13, 2022. https://www.officedepot.com/l/credit/compare?cm_sp=marketing-_-FooterAds-Credit-_-Footer-Ads-Ad2-Footer%3Fcm_sp.
5. *Shipping boxes, shipping supplies, packaging materials, packing supplies.* ULINE. (n.d.). Retrieved December 13, 2022, from https://www.uline.com/
6. *Grainger Industrial Supply - MRO products, equipment and Tools.* Grainger Industrial Supply - MRO Products, Equipment and Tools. (n.d.). Retrieved December 13, 2022, from https://www.grainger.com/
7. ECREDABLE pricing. eCredable Small Business. (n.d.). Retrieved December 13, 2022, from https://business.ecredable.com/Pricing
8. *Creditstrong business - get a business credit builder loan.* Credit Strong. (2022, July 15). Retrieved December 13, 2022, from https://www.creditstrong.com/business/

5. MONITOR BUSINESS CREDIT REPORTS

1. *Consumer Portal.* LexisNexis. (n.d.). Retrieved December 13, 2022, from https://consumer.risk.lexisnexis.com/request
2. *Request ChexSystems consumer disclosure report.* ChexSystems. (n.d.). Retrieved December 13, 2022, from https://www.chexsystems.com/request-reports/consumer-disclosure
3. Davies, A. (2020, April 28). *What is credit monitoring and is it effective?* American Express Credit Cards, Rewards & Banking. Retrieved November 4, 2022, from https://www.americanexpress.com/en-us/credit-cards/credit-intel/credit-monitoring/
4. *Submit a complaint.* Consumer Financial Protection Bureau. (n.d.). Retrieved December 13, 2022, from https://www.consumerfinance.gov/complaint/

5. *National Association of Consumer Advocates.* NACA. (n.d.). Retrieved December 13, 2022, from https://www.consumeradvocates.org/
6. Wells, L. (n.d.). *How to clear up your ChexSystems record.* Bankrate. Retrieved December 13, 2022, from https://www.bankrate.com/banking/how-to-clear-up-chexsystems-report/#second-chance-account

6. BUILDING TIER 2 CREDIT

1. Square Biz. (2022, March 17). *The best way to get tier 2 net 30 accounts.* YouTube. Retrieved December 14, 2022, from https://www.youtube.com/watch?v=cojsQ0W8lpE

8. TIER 4: HIGH-LIMIT CASH LINES OF

1. Admin. (2022, February 17). *VC funding: 7 rules to secure funding for startups.* 7 startup. Retrieved December 14, 2022, from https://www.7startup.vc/post/vc-funding-7-rules-to-secure-funding-for-startups/

9. BUSINESS LOANS

1. *Write your business plan.* Small Business Administration. (n.d.). Retrieved December 14, 2022, from https://www.sba.gov/business-guide/plan-your-business/write-your-business-plan
2. Furgison, L. (2020, March 3). *How to secure a business loan: Tips from a banking executive.* Bplans Blog. Retrieved December 14, 2022, from https://articles.bplans.com/how-to-secure-a-business-loan-tips-from-a-banking-executive/